TO:

FROM:

DATE:

The MIRACLE OF EASTER

A 40-DAY REFLECTION ON THE RESURRECTION OF CHRIST

by

CHRIS TIEGREEN

Christian Art
PUBLISHERS

Visit Christian Art Gifts, Inc., at www.christianartgifts.com.

The Miracle of Easter: A 40-Day Reflection on the Resurrection of Christ

Previously published by Tyndale Momentum under the title *The Promise of Lent Devotional: A 40-day Journey toward the Miracle of Easter.* Copyright © 2017.

Published by Christian Art Gifts, Inc., Bloomingdale, IL, USA under license from Tyndale House Publishers, Inc.

First edition 2025.

Designed by Christian Art Gifts, Inc.

Cover and interior images used under license from Shutterstock.com.

Most Christian Art titles may be purchased at bulk discounts by churches, nonprofits, and corporations. For more information, please email SpecialMarkets@cagifts.com.

ISBN 979-8-89678-192-9

Printed in China.

30 29 28 27 26 25
10 9 8 7 6 5 4 3 2 1

For Hannah

Lent is a time

of transition, when we

turn our eyes away from

fading disappointments

and toward the brilliant

promises of God.

INTRODUCTION

MANY EARLY CHRISTIANS prepared to commemorate the death and resurrection of Jesus with a season of repentance. Their practices varied widely from place to place and from time to time, but by the fourth century, the idea of spending forty days in preparation for Easter had crystallized into common practice. This Lenten season became a time of sobering reflection—on sins, on the death and decay of a world gone wrong, and on the hopeless condition we would be in without the intervention of God in Christ. Believers were encouraged to feel the full weight of these concepts by expressing repentance and denying themselves. It is perhaps the most solemn time of year for many Christians.

Lent is not meant to be depressing; however, it is meant to be reorienting.

Repentance is never an end in itself in God's Kingdom; it always leads to joy. It is an entry point into a new way of seeing, the beginning of an inner transformation that changes our vision and the direction of our lives. It may remind us of our disappointments for a moment, but it is meant to move us quickly into the light, where our eyes are filled with awe, wonder, and anticipation. Even the most sober-minded believer contemplating the themes of Lent realizes the ways God has turned them all toward his glory and our ultimate good. When we gaze at his true nature, everything changes. The past fades away, and our hearts are filled with hope.

That is the purpose of this devotional: to stir up the hope that God has given us in the midst of a fallen world. As believers, we are in continual transition between the trauma of the old creation and the glories of the new. We may feel the full weight of the old for a time, but it is temporary. The new will last forever. Lent is a time of transition, when we turn our eyes away from fading disappointments and toward the brilliant promises of God.

You will see many contrasting themes of the Lent and Easter season in these readings: death and resurrection, decay versus growth and life, frailty and weakness becoming strength, temptation and the power to overcome it, temporality versus eternity, the old genesis and the new creation, our helplessness and God's provision, our faults under his forgiveness and mercy, and humanity's rebellion of pride versus Jesus' victory of humility. In many cases, these are more than a difference in perspective; they are issues we wrestle with every day.

This devotional follows the Lent calendar most commonly used in the United States, beginning on Ash Wednesday and ending on the Saturday between Good Friday and Easter, with Sundays celebrated as resurrection "breaks" in the forty-day period. Each reading is based on a brief biblical passage and is followed by a prayer, some reflection questions and thoughts, and a related quote from the church's long tradition of Lenten and Easter music. The prayers are simple, but if you will go through the process of sincerely voicing them, you will find God answering in subtle and sometimes not-so-subtle ways. Your times of reflection, even if brief, can be genuinely life-transforming.

Throughout these readings, let yourself both feel the experiences of the first Holy Week and see the big picture of God's redemptive plan. The "micro" perspective puts your senses into the story; the "macro" will inspire you with the enormity of it all. This season is a special time on the calendar and certainly more than a ritual. It's a time to experience the wisdom and mercies of God. May he fill your heart, mind, and spirit with the fullness of his presence each day.

Ash Wednesday

— DAY 1 —

CREATURES *of* DUST

GENESIS 3:17-19

You were made from dust, and to dust you will return.

GENESIS 3:19

THE HUMAN HEART is full of eternal hopes. Many people don't recognize them for what they are—longings for the Kingdom of Heaven and anticipation of living with God and his people forever—but everyone dreams. We were designed for such things; God put eternity in our hearts for a reason (Ecclesiastes 3:11). We *ought* to be filled with hope. But in spite of all our longings and desires, in spite of all the promises we have been given, Scripture reminds us of a fundamental truth from its earliest pages:

We are made of dust. And, as a consequence of humanity's primeval rebellion, to dust we will return.

Scripture portrays our creation from dust and explains why we must return to it, but even without reading its explanations we know the fact of our mortal condition. We are painfully jolted into awareness at every funeral and nagged with a reminder at every ache and pain that comes with age. We may be able to put our transient nature out of our minds for a surprisingly long time, especially when we're young, but eventually the quickening years overcome our denial. Like Abraham, we come face-to-face with God and are reminded of our materiality (Genesis 18:27). We know our innermost beings were made for more, but our outermost will return to earth. It's inevitable.

That thought has plagued humanity for centuries and driven many to despair. For those who believe in the Messiah who came to save us, however, it is merely a reminder of what our fate would have been without him. It's a remnant of the fall, not a lasting legacy. We have no reason to be depressed anymore—not because we have overcome death and decay but because he has. The season of Lent is not a lamentation with no answer; it's a reflection on what could have been but isn't, a sobering celebration of how tragic losses are being redeemed. For the heart of faith, Lent reflections take the "bitter" out of bittersweet while reminding us it was there.

That's a healthy balance. We don't want to dwell on the painful side of redemption constantly; the gospel places a heavy emphasis on celebration and joy. But we're always grateful for what the Messiah's sacrifice saved us from and mindful of what it cost him. Our broken bodies came from dust and will return to it. But our true selves—the people we were created to be—will rejoice forever.

— PRAYER —

Lord, remind me of my frail condition during this season. Remind me even more of how you overcame it. May this be a time of deep repentance and even deeper gratitude. Amen.

REFLECTION

How often do you think about your mortality? In what ways can those thoughts encourage your faith rather than undermine it?

Further reading: Ecclesiastes 3:18-20

When once I must depart, do not depart from me;
when I must suffer death, then stand thou by me.

"ST. MATTHEW PASSION," JOHANN SEBASTIAN BACH, WORDS BY CHRISTIAN FRIEDRICH HENRICI (PICANDER)

Thursday

— DAY 2 —

OUT *of* FUTILITY

ROMANS 8:18-21

Against its will, all creation was subjected to God's curse.

ROMANS 8:20

THE WORLD LIES under a curse of futility. We've not only noticed that; we've experienced the frustration ourselves. Sometimes our plans work out, and we love it when they do, but disappointment is a universal phenomenon. We lament the challenges we face, and we might implicitly or explicitly accuse God of letting us down—as if he were personally opposed to our sense of satisfaction—even when we know that isn't the case. It's as if Eden were a secret garden that we think we might have glimpsed from time to time. But the walls are high, and we can never find the gate. Life as we want it to be is always just out of reach.

Creation was subjected to a curse because of humanity's rebellion—not primarily as a punishment but as a consequence. God had to let us feel the weight of the Fall and experience the results of our independence from him. Otherwise, we might be content in our rebellion and never cry out for a Savior. We would miss out on the reason we were created and never know the Creator. We would be alive without ever really living.

So God subjected the world to frustration, and today we long for the fullness of our redemption. We live in a world that is marred by deterioration and decay, in spite of humanity's efforts to prop it up, whitewash its problems, and give it the appearance of flourishing. Through the cracks of this world's facade, we still see mountains of poverty and injustice, pain and suffering, disease and desperation. But we are masters of illusion, and we willingly attend our own show. We distract ourselves in a world of our making while trying to turn it into a better place.

God does not intend to make the world better; he intends

to make it new. His Kingdom is not earth's home-improvement project but a radical renovation. The Messiah establishes a new government. The Incarnation is his charter document, the Cross his signature in blood, the Resurrection his cultural manifesto. Old things are passing away; new things have come. The Garden of Eden may be out of reach, but the city of God is not. The curse has been broken.

Remember that in this season. We were bound in futility but are now unbound. Though we embrace the solemnity of redemption in a fallen world, the promise looms larger. And every day is an opportunity to experience it more fully.

— PRAYER —

Lord, thank you for breaking the curse of futility.
Lead me into fullness of joy. I want to experience
every dimension of the promises you have given—
for this age and the age to come. Amen.

REFLECTION

In what ways have you experienced the futility of the world? In what ways do you experience the fullness of the Kingdom? How can you participate in God's "renovation" program for the world?

Further reading: 2 Corinthians 5:17-19

The morning purples all the sky,
The air with praises rings;
Defeated hell stands sullen by,
The world exulting sings.

"THE MORNING PURPLES ALL THE SKY,"
SAINT AMBROSE OF MILAN

Friday

— DAY 3 —

CITIZENS *of* GLORY

ROMANS 8:18-21

What we suffer now is nothing compared to the glory he will reveal to us later.

ROMANS 8:18

When a person seeks citizenship in a new country, he or she is usually required to renounce allegiance to the old one. Why? Because sometimes the national interests of different countries are in conflict. No country is well served by the double-minded. Loyalties must be clearly stated.

Those who have entered into a relationship with Christ live in two realms and, for a time, have dual citizenship. But we can retain our loyalty to only one, the world or the Kingdom, because their interests stand in conflict with each other.

Much of the Christian life is framed by this conflict; we are constantly having to forsake the old way of life for the new, envision our future and put away our past, and embrace the culture of the Kingdom over the culture of the world and its ways. The realm we see with our physical eyes is subject to death and decay. The realm we see with the eyes of faith is not. Every moment of every day we face a choice: Which realm will we live in, invest in, place our hopes in, and cultivate in ourselves and in the lives of those around us? The choices are rarely easy. It takes time to learn a new way of life.

In the process, we are acutely aware that we are still suffering the effects of a fallen world, no matter how much our hearts long for the unfallen Kingdom. We encounter the pain and frustration of exile from Eden, from original design, from the image of God we are created to carry. "Creation looks forward to the day when it will join God's children in glorious freedom from death and decay," Paul writes (verse 21), because death and decay are still present. Our loyalties may be clearly on the side of the uncorrupted Kingdom, yet our experience is still mixed. Redemption has been freely given but not completely fulfilled. For now, we still hurt sometimes.

As we reflect on the Cross and Resurrection—the exodus from one citizenship into another—we need to keep resolutely focused on the coming glory. It does not and cannot compare to the pain we face today. We have the promise that the benefits of God's Kingdom always outweigh the costs, even when the costs are excruciating. Hold on to that promise; it will become extremely precious in times of crisis. You are called to celebrate the revelation of the coming Kingdom long before you see it. Your new citizenship is far more glorious than your old.

— PRAYER —

Lord, just as Jesus lived from heaven into earth's realm, may I live from spiritual realities while walking in the visible world. Give me revelations of hope, and fill me with visions of the coming glory. Amen.

REFLECTION

Why is it important to remember that the glory we are promised outweighs the pain we experience? How does focusing on our citizenship in God's Kingdom change how we live?

Further reading: 2 Corinthians 5:6-8

The heavenly land I see,
With peace and plenty blest;
A land of sacred liberty,
And endless rest.

"THE GOD OF ABRAHAM PRAISE," THOMAS OLIVERS
ADAPTED FROM "YIGDAL" BY DANIEL BEN JUDAH

Saturday

— DAY 4 —

A CHOICE *of* REALMS

MATTHEW 4:1-4

Jesus was led by the Spirit into the wilderness to be tempted there by the devil. For forty days and forty nights he fasted and became very hungry.

MATTHEW 4:1-2

JESUS HAD JUST BEEN dramatically affirmed at his baptism by open heavens, the descent of the dove, and a voice from heaven. "This is my dearly loved Son, who brings me great joy," the voice said (Matthew 3:17), affirming Jesus' true identity and announcing his unique nature to all who heard. It was a glorious moment, full of God's presence and assurance.

The very next verse tells us that the Spirit sent Jesus into a harsh wilderness where he would be tempted, as he fasted for forty days. That's a remarkably grim assignment for a Son who has delighted the Father, but it was necessary. Jesus came not only to redeem us from the fallenness of the world but to overcome it. He could not be Lord and Master if the world's impulses and pleasures or the enemy's tempting voice had mastered him. So he went, he endured, and he overcame. He demonstrated decisively that he was rooted not in a fading world but in another realm.

The season of Lent echoes this call to forsake impulses and fleeting desires because we, as followers of Jesus, must also demonstrate that we are rooted in another realm. The flesh itself is not evil. God created it and declared it good, and he promised a bodily resurrection. This material world and our physical bodies exist by God's design. But the body does need to be reminded that it is not our essence. Fasting makes a statement to the flesh, along with all its distorted cravings, that it does not rule us and cannot hold us forever. Self-denial says *no* to something material in order to say *yes* to something much deeper and long-lasting.

We don't earn spiritual points for self-denial; in fact, some people focus so intently on denying the flesh that they actually affirm its power. But fasting, in its various forms, does remind us which Kingdom sustains us. It turns our attention to the deeper realities of our lives and the Father who breathes into us. It's a statement of allegiance to the realm of the Spirit, an effective exercise in saying no to the immediate for the sake of the eternal.

Many people make that statement in one form or another during the forty days of Lent, and it can have a profound spiritual impact. It is worth our unyielding persistence. The more we become aware that we are rooted in another realm, the more we begin to experience it.

— PRAYER —

Father, help me to know my roots—my citizenship in your Kingdom and my dependence on your Spirit. Lead me not into temptation, but grant me the strength to overcome it, with Jesus, in every form I encounter it. Amen.

REFLECTION

In what ways does giving something up for Lent direct our attention to the spiritual realm? Why is it valuable to be reminded of our "temptability"? How does temptation—and overcoming it—help us identify with Jesus and bond with him relationally?

Further reading: Hebrews 4:15-16

His strength shall bear thy spirit up,
And brace thy heart and nerve thine arm.

"TAKE UP THY CROSS," CHARLES W. EVEREST

FIRST SUNDAY *of* LENT

In fact, Christ has been raised from the dead. He is the first of a great harvest of all who have died. So you see, just as death came into the world through a man, now the resurrection from the dead has begun through another man. Just as everyone dies because we all belong to Adam, everyone who belongs to Christ will be given new life. But there is an order to this resurrection: Christ was raised as the first of the harvest; then all who belong to Christ will be raised when he comes back.

1 CORINTHIANS 15:20-23

— PRAYER —

My God and my Father, every judgment of yours is trimmed with hope; every lamentation of mine is framed by your promises; every heartbreak leads to your joy. Thank you that even in this season of Lent, our solemnity is punctuated by six reminders of the resurrection, six Sundays until our resurrection day comes. Fill my heart with your goodness on each of them, and every day between. Amen.

Long my imprisoned spirit lay,
Fast bound in sin and nature's night;
Thine eye diffused a quickening ray;
I woke—the dungeon flamed with light!
My chains fell off, my heart was free,
I rose, went forth, and followed Thee.

"AND CAN IT BE, THAT I SHOULD GAIN?" CHARLES WESLEY

Monday

— DAY 5 —

A CHANGED MIND

MARK 1:9-15

"The time has come," he said. "The kingdom of God has come near. Repent and believe the good news!"

MARK 1:15, NIV

REPENT AND *BELIEVE* are often considered the first words of the gospel because, according to Mark, Jesus began his public preaching ministry with them. The second word inspires us; we long to be filled with mountain-moving faith. But repentance? That's more intimidating. We know the connotations. It has been thundered from high pulpits and shouted from street platforms for centuries, resonating with shame-filled hearts and offending the proud. Repentance is a true command; Jesus and Scripture would not emphasize it if it were not. But the command comes with such baggage that we have to wonder if centuries of voices have translated it well.

Hebraic tradition emphasized the behavioral side of repentance, and Greek thought emphasized a renewed understanding, though both originate inside of us and have outward consequences. But regardless of how we dissect repentance, we can be certain God means it comprehensively. It has to go deep. And there's only one way for that to happen—not through disciplining our outward selves, but by learning a radically different way to see.

Lent is not a time to beat yourself up. It's a time to immerse yourself in a new way of seeing. That's the kind of repentance that aligns with God's purposes for you and that ultimately produces lasting change. When you see with new eyes, you don't have to train yourself to do the right things. Your inward transformation shapes your outward expression.

So what does Jesus want us to see? The astonishingly good news that his Kingdom is near—accessible, recognizable, and available for us to experience. That's the focus of his preaching and the reason he tells us to repent. In order to know and experience him, we have to be able to see extraordinary Kingdom realities. But jaded minds are skeptical of such good news; we have to repent to embrace it.

We live in a world that is in a state of disorganization, deterioration, and decay. But the Kingdom, which begins as imperceptibly as a mustard seed, will overcome the world. This Kingdom flourishes. It's full of life. It grows. A mind steeped in the world and its disappointments will miss Kingdom truth. It believes without really trusting and hopes without really expecting. The repentance for which Jesus calls changes that weary perspective and replaces it with the vision to see the truth: an unfolding promise of goodness and glory. The Kingdom really has come near. Turn your perspective away from old ways of seeing and embrace the new. Then walk in the vision you've been given.

— PRAYER —

Lord, during this Lenten season, divorce me from my dependence on what I see. Give me eyes to see the glory of your Kingdom each day, and teach me to walk in it. Amen.

REFLECTION

In practical terms, what is the difference between a changed mind and changed behavior? How are they related? Is it possible to have one without the other? Why or why not?

Further reading: Luke 13:18-19

Our hearts be pure from evil,
That we may see aright
The Lord in rays eternal
Of resurrection light.

"THE DAY OF RESURRECTION," JOHN OF DAMASCUS

Tuesday

— DAY 6 —

A SACRED VESSEL

2 CORINTHIANS 4:5-7

We now have this light shining in our hearts, but we ourselves are like fragile clay jars containing this great treasure.

2 CORINTHIANS 4:7

IF WE EVER WANTED a clear picture of how the realm of the spirit intersects with the material world, we need look no further than Jesus. The Incarnation was a restatement of who we were originally designed to be: dust of the earth formed into flesh and filled with the breath of God. That's the picture we get from Eden, and nowhere has God said, "Never mind." Jesus came as the exact image of God—our original design—and lived as we were supposed to live. He restored the pattern. He presented a portrait of the divine breath inside of a physical body destined for glory.

We, of course, live in corruptible flesh, but we are redeemed and restored to offer the same picture to the world. We are material bodies filled with the Spirit of God, fragile jars of clay filled with a great treasure, creatures of dust carrying a dazzling light. Sometimes—very often, in fact—that light is obscured beyond recognition, the treasure hidden deep inside. But it is there. Much of the Christian life is a matter of letting the Spirit shine through us. This divine light, freely available by faith, is given to us in order to be revealed.

The world longs for such a revelation (Romans 8:19), yet we are reluctant to claim that we have it. We focus instead on our frailties, faults, and fallenness. There is a time for that—Lent is one such occasion for healthy introspection and repentance—but it should always point us away from the problem and toward God's glorious solution: the habitation of his Spirit within these material vessels. That's where weakness becomes strength, faults are covered with mercy, pride gives way to humility, decay is overtaken by life, and the temporal is clothed in the eternal. In other words, our fragile jars of clay are a brilliant showcase for God.

Don't be afraid to live as that showcase. Be humble, of course—it's him in you, not just you alone—but you have been given an opportunity to reveal the character and nature of God to the world. Let the light shining in your heart scatter its rays into other hearts around you. Cultivate your treasure and share it freely.

— PRAYER —

Holy Spirit of God, fill this vessel of clay with overflowing treasure. Overcome the brokenness of my flesh with the wholeness of your wisdom, power, and love. Amen.

REFLECTION

In what ways might seeing yourself as a sacred vessel of God's glory change how you relate to other people?

Further reading: 2 Peter 1:3-4

King of glory, soul of bliss, Alleluia!
Everlasting life is this, Alleluia!
Thee to know, thy power to prove, Alleluia!
Thus to sing, and thus to love, Alleluia!

"CHRIST THE LORD IS RISEN TODAY," CHARLES WESLEY

Wednesday

— DAY 7 —

A PURPOSEFUL DEATH

2 CORINTHIANS 4:8-10

Through suffering, our bodies continue to share in the death of Jesus so that the life of Jesus may also be seen in our bodies.

2 CORINTHIANS 4:10

We were made for glory. We know that; we can feel it in the depths of our hearts. The desire is embedded in the spiritual DNA we were given long ago. But every day we also face the painful reality of the world as we know it. Glory is faint and fleeting in this world, and the world's ways of searching for it are ultimately futile. We're trapped between longing and experience, and there seems to be no way out except death.

Until Jesus. We know the Easter story, how he died for

us so we could live for him. He willingly took the sources of all the world's futility onto his shoulders and carried them to the cross. The primeval rebellion, the sins of the ages, the pride of human hearts—all of it went into the grave, and none of it came out with him. The free gift of salvation, our redemption and restoration from a fallen existence, is a beautiful promise. Nothing we can do will earn or merit this promise. There's nothing left for us but gratitude.

Or is there? Clearly we cannot earn our redemption and restoration, but is there some way to position ourselves to experience it more fully? Paul seemed to think so. The treasure we carry in these earthen vessels can only come out if the earthen vessels are broken. We cannot live from the strength of our own flesh and still experience the strength of the Spirit. One of them must rule while the other fades into the background. Which will it be? This season of introspection, repentance, and discipline reminds us of the choice we made when we believed in Jesus. We must enter into his death in order to experience his life. The grime on the windows of our souls must be washed away, our material trappings stripped off to expose the light within. The more we die, the more we live.

We are not called simply to believe the Cross but also to participate in it. No, we won't die as Jesus did, providing a sacrifice for all. But we will die; in fact, we are in the process now. But even more, we are in the process of experiencing new life that lasts forever. And that life will forever be full of the glory we were designed to share.

— PRAYER —

Lord, may your treasure in me be clearly seen. In my weakness, show your strength. In my helplessness, show your provision and power. In my futility, show your victory. And in my death, show your life. Amen.

REFLECTION

What does it mean to be crucified and resurrected with Jesus? What implications does that have for our lives today?

Further reading: Romans 6:3-11

Yea! Gladly is the flesh and blood in us
Compelled to the Cross;
The more it benefits our souls, the more painfully it weighs.

"ST. MATTHEW PASSION," JOHANN SEBASTIAN BACH,
WORDS BY CHRISTIAN FRIEDRICH HENRICI (PICANDER)

Thursday

— DAY 8 —

A TRANSFORMING VISION

2 CORINTHIANS 4:16-18

We don't look at the troubles we can see now; rather,

we fix our gaze on things that cannot be seen.

2 CORINTHIANS 4:18

OUR GAZE determines the direction of our lives. The vision we hold in front of us is the one that steers us. We become what we behold. We are told such things by today's self-help guides, as if they had discovered some long-lost secret to human behavior. But the truth is already in the Scriptures, and it has been playing out for all of human history. God gave Abraham a visual picture of his descendants, and Abraham believed. He gave Joseph a dream, and Joseph eventually experienced it. He had David anointed with promise, and David eventually stepped into it. The pattern has been repeated with all sorts of judges, prophets, priests, kings, and regular people outside the spotlight, and it shapes our lives today. What we look at matters.

Paul expressed this concept in his second letter to the Corinthians: "We all, with unveiled face, beholding the glory of the Lord, are being transformed into the same image from one degree of glory to another" (2 Corinthians 3:18, ESV). If we want to be transformed into the image of Christ, we must gaze at Christ. If we want to see heavenly realities, we must take our eyes off of earthly ones. If we want to leave the ways of the flesh behind us, we must stop focusing on the flesh and instead walk in the Spirit (Galatians 5:16). We never escape our problems by staring at them. We can only move on by replacing old visions with new ones.

We might be frustrated by instructions that tell us to gaze at things that cannot be seen, but this is what the life of faith is all about. The issue isn't so much what we see but which lenses we choose to look through. Circumstances look different through eyes of faith than they do through natural vision. God's promises become our ultimate interpreters. If our perspective does not line up with the fullness and the glory of what he has said, we have to change it. There is no other way to experience his Kingdom in this world.

Of all the disciplines you seek to impose on yourself, let this one be your priority. With every circumstance, ask God how he sees it. Then align yourself with his vision. He is never pessimistic or fearful, so you will find yourself filled with hope and confidence. Stubbornly and relentlessly, look into eternity. Your troubles will begin to look impotent, and faith will fill your heart.

— PRAYER —

Holy Spirit, reorient my vision to see how you see.
Give me the perseverance to look past the surface
of my life and into your behind-the-scenes purposes.
May visions of eternity guide my every step. Amen.

REFLECTION

Why does it take discipline to see in new ways? What perspectives do you think you most need to change?

Further reading: Isaiah 55:8-9

Bane and blessing, pain and pleasure,
By the cross are sanctified;
Peace is there that knows no measure,
Joys that through all time abide.

"IN THE CROSS OF CHRIST I GLORY," JOHN BOWRING

Friday

— DAY 9 —

A CONFIDENT LONGING

2 CORINTHIANS 5:1-5

We grow weary in our present bodies, and we long to put on our heavenly bodies like new clothing.

2 CORINTHIANS 5:2

PAUL HAD PLENTY of reasons to be weary in his body. He had been beaten numerous times, sometimes with whips and sometimes with bone-crushing rods. He traveled thousands of miles, had been stoned and left for dead, was shipwrecked three times, and spent long periods of time in prison cells and chains. He had been without food and drink, and he knew the extremes of cold and heat (2 Corinthians 11:23-27). His body had been through a lot.

Paul showed no inclinations to build a nice life and avoid

the world's troubles. In fact, he leaned into them. Much as an airplane heads into the wind to rise above it, many zealous servants of God throughout the centuries have willingly walked into moments of crisis rather than away from them. Yes, they grew weary in their physical bodies, but they knew a much deeper truth: The trials of the world never outlast the promises of the Kingdom. Suffering is temporary; glory is eternal. And the former often provides unusual opportunities for the latter.

In our season of preparation for Passion Week, we lean into the ache and heartbreak of this world rather than trying to flee from it. We do so for several reasons: to follow in the footsteps of our Savior, to obey his command to deny ourselves, to remind ourselves of what we've been delivered from, and to plant our feet firmly in the Kingdom we've chosen. These are profound statements for us to make, but often they happen not as results of our choosing but as the results of time and circumstances. We are blessed for claiming them willingly, but even when we don't, we are blessed for responding to the pain with hope. The eyes of faith look toward heaven and eternity, even—or especially—when life hurts.

People without perspective have nothing but complaints for the trials of this age. People with heavenly vision have nothing but anticipation. We already know Jesus has overcome the world, and for that we carry an unusual—and, in the eyes of others, unreasonable—kind of joy. That joy is a remarkable testimony in a culture that rarely knows what to do with its pain. When we in these earthly tents look with confidence toward our heavenly dwelling, we become living witnesses to redemption, restoration, and the promise of the Kingdom.

— PRAYER —

Lord, grant that I would be such a witness.
Strengthen me to endure suffering,
give me courage to lean into life's trials, and make
my face radiate with the promises of eternity. Amen.

REFLECTION

Why do you think suffering drives some people away from God and draws others to him? What statement does our hope make to people who don't have an eternal perspective?

Further reading: John 16:33

Hark! How the heav'nly anthem
drowns all music but its own.

"CROWN HIM WITH MANY CROWNS,"
MATTHEW BRIDGES AND GODFREY THRING

Saturday

— DAY 10 —

A GRATEFUL RESPONSE

HEBREWS 13:10-16

Let us offer through Jesus a continual sacrifice of praise to God, proclaiming our allegiance to his name.

HEBREWS 13:15

JESUS SUFFERED "outside the city gates" (verse 12) in order to fulfill his role as our sacrifice. Not only is that image loaded with sacred symbolism; it's also loaded with meaning for those of us who follow in his footsteps. The writer of Hebrews uses Jesus' sacrifice outside the city to parallel our discipleship. Christ offered himself; so do we. He did not try to fit into the world's ways; neither should we. He endured the pain and suffering of the cross for "the joy awaiting him" (Hebrews 12:2); so must we. We're given every reason to enjoy the goodness of God in this world, but we can't afford to invest our entire lives in its fleeting conditions. "This world is not our permanent home; we are looking forward to a home yet to come" (13:14). We must be willing to be marginalized in this age in order to experience the fullness of the Kingdom. Just like Jesus.

The beauty of this passage in Hebrews, and of this gospel as a whole, is that it unites sacrifice with praise, temporary rejection with an eternal home, and suffering with glory. While many people pity Christians for being out of touch, self-deprived, or some other lamentable condition, we embrace these very things as our stepping-stones into the riches of the Kingdom. Where many see rough-hewn rocks, we see diamonds waiting to be cut and polished. Though some avoid servanthood at all costs, we see it as a path to greatness. While some see childlikeness as immaturity, we see it as the key to spiritual power. Yes, our values look skewed to a watching world, but only because they don't fit into a false system. In the Kingdom, they are truth that lasts.

Seek fellowship and love in this world, but don't be afraid to be found "outside the city" at times. This is a fitting response of gratitude and praise for the one who died outside the city for us. Being in his Kingdom comes at a cost, but it also comes with far greater rewards—in this age *and* the age to come (Luke 18:29-30). However difficult life in this world becomes for you, continually lift up a sacrifice of praise to God. When you do, you are not only declaring your loyalty to him; you are embracing the values of his Kingdom. And you will never be outside the gates of his city.

— PRAYER —

Whether I feel like I belong in this world or not, Lord, I know I belong in your Kingdom. For that, I praise you from the depths of my heart, today and forever. Amen.

REFLECTION

In what ways, if any, does your citizenship in heaven make you uncomfortable in this world? What do you think it means to offer Jesus a "sacrifice of praise"?

Further reading: 1 Peter 2:9-12

No human heart could ever now imagine
What it should give thee.

"ST. JOHN PASSION," JOHANN SEBASTIAN BACH,
WORDS ANONYMOUS

SECOND SUNDAY *of* LENT

It is the same way with the resurrection of the dead. Our earthly bodies are planted in the ground when we die, but they will be raised to live forever. Our bodies are buried in brokenness, but they will be raised in glory. They are buried in weakness, but they will be raised in strength. They are buried as natural human bodies, but they will be raised as spiritual bodies. For just as there are natural bodies, there are also spiritual bodies. The Scriptures tell us, "The first man, Adam, became a living person." But the last Adam—that is, Christ—is a life-giving Spirit. What comes first is the natural body, then the spiritual body comes later. Adam, the first man, was made from the dust of the earth, while Christ, the second man, came from heaven. Earthly people are like the earthly man, and heavenly people are like the heavenly man. Just as we are now like the earthly man, we will someday be like the heavenly man.

1 CORINTHIANS 15:42-49

— PRAYER —

Lord, everything you created is important, including this material world and my physical body. But I know what is most important and what lasts forever. Teach me to sow my weakness, my brokenness, my material possessions, and my natural form into the soil of your Kingdom, and may the seeds I have sown flourish and bear eternal fruit. Amen.

O, ye who in cold graves are sleeping, in eternal sleep deep in its grasp holds fast, henceforth awake to joy and bliss.

"CHRIST ON THE MOUNT OF OLIVES,"
LUDWIG VAN BEETHOVEN, WORDS BY FRANZ XAVER HUBER

Monday

— DAY 11 —

A CLEAN HEART

PSALM 51:7-12

Create in me a clean heart, O God.

Renew a loyal spirit within me.

PSALM 51:10

MOST OF US are well aware of God's promises of forgiveness, but letting them sink into our hearts is another matter. Regardless of how much he assures us that he has separated our sins from us—as far as the east is from the west, he says (Psalm 103:12)—something in us feels the need to revisit them. At one level, we want to be completely free of our sins without any cost. But we intuitively sense that freedom can only come when we embrace guilt and pay the price. Contrite hearts are filled with the impulse to make things right.

Guilt and shame are terrible burdens to bear, and our efforts to compensate would never be enough to free ourselves. Yes, we need to make restitution for offenses, but that's for restoration, not cleansing. Only a divine work and a perfect sacrifice can bear the full weight of our burden. Until we have fully embraced the free gift of atonement, we will struggle under the load. A nagging voice will remind us of how we've failed. Shame will haunt us. And we have no escape on our own.

It is important in seasons of reflection not only to feel the weight of sin but to realize how fully the Son of God absorbed it. He does not ask us to carry even a small portion of it. Grief can lead to confession and repentance (2 Corinthians 7:8-11), but that's where it should end. Scripture never mentions the sadness of salvation, only its joy. We have divine permission—even a mandate—to get past our self-inflicted pain and celebrate his blessings. He is a restorer, a rebuilder, and a reformer. He wants us to be free.

The problem for us imperfect creatures is that we will

likely face our own sinfulness again, maybe even today. Not all of our sins are in the past. But according to the gospel, they are already in the grave, and they will stay there. We now live in the Resurrection, even when our old eyes see evidence to the contrary. We choose to see the new.

Let yourself feel the weight of redemption this Lenten season, but feel the weight as it fell on Jesus, not on yourself. You are free from it. That's a sobering thought that leads to gratitude, not guilt. Pray David's prayer in Psalm 51, and believe its promise. God really does cleanse hearts and restore joy. Never let guilt or shame stand in the way of that.

— PRAYER —

Father, my prayer is like David's: that you would give me a clean heart and restore the joy of my salvation. You never reject a broken and repentant heart, and I offer you mine. Amen.

REFLECTION

Why is it important to grieve sins and realize the cost of salvation? Why is it important not to try to carry the weight of sin yourself? How has God addressed both concerns?

Further reading: 1 John 1:5-9

O come, come, embrace me; for without you my
heart is completely orphaned and wretched.

"EASTER ORATORIO," JOHANN SEBASTIAN BACH,
WORDS BY CHRISTIAN FRIEDRICH HENRICI (PICANDER)

Tuesday

— DAY 12 —

WHEN MORNING COMES

LAMENTATIONS 3:18-24

The faithful love of the LORD never ends!

His mercies never cease. Great is his faithfulness;

his mercies begin afresh each morning.

LAMENTATIONS 3:22-23

THE HISTORICAL CONTEXT of the book of Lamentations is the fall of Jerusalem and the destruction of the Temple by the Babylonians. God's covenant people were not unaccustomed to divine discipline or the idea that they had failed his covenant at times, but the thought that he would let his own people be taken captive and his own dwelling place be destroyed was unfathomable. Even in their rebellion—their sins, injustices, idolatry, and other expressions of unfaithfulness—the Israelites expected him to deliver them from danger, especially danger from the thoroughly ungodly Babylonians. As Jerusalem and its Temple lay in ruins, and as many of its leaders and young men and women were carried off into captivity, the air was filled with hopelessness and despair. Even tears couldn't express the sense of utter devastation.

That description fits Jerusalem six centuries before Jesus, but it points to a much larger picture. We also lament the loss of what could have been—the blessings we were given at Creation and the catastrophic way we forfeited them when we rebelled against God. The story of Israel and Judah is the story of us all. We carried God's image within us. Given the opportunity to know him, experience the fullness of his presence, hear his voice clearly, and receive his love without hindrance, we turned to less worthy loves and ignored his desires for us. We had everything and messed it up. That's the story of humanity.

In some form or another, it's also the individual story we each share. We lost innocence somewhere along the way, became our own lords, and began writing the plot of our own lives. Despite our best efforts, they have all taken tragic turns. Like the prophet, we cry out, "My splendor is gone! Everything I had hoped for from the LORD is lost!" (verse 18). But the message of the gospel is that God does not leave us in our lament. He bought us back, has restored our relationship with him, and fills our mouths with words of gratitude. His faithfulness never ends and his mercies are new every morning. Every day is the beginning of a new life.

Wake up each morning with that perspective. Put the pain of the past behind you. The Resurrection was a one-time event, but its power applies yesterday, today, and tomorrow. Our laments were not meant to last. No life given to Christ continues to lie in ruins. Whatever we lost can be, and will be, restored.

— PRAYER —

Lord, I know the pain of regret, and I wish I could live some parts of my life over again—or at least undo some of my decisions. Thank you for redemption and your promise of restoration. May I never miss another blessing you have planned for me. Amen.

REFLECTION

To what degree do you live with a sense of regret? How does God's promise of deliverance and restoration heal the pains of your past?

Further reading: Philippians 3:13-14

When morning gilds the skies,
my heart awaking cries:
May Jesus Christ be praised!

"WHEN MORNING GILDS THE SKIES," GERMAN HYMN

Wednesday

— DAY 13 —

FAITH WAITS

LAMENTATIONS 3:25-30

It is good to wait quietly

for salvation from the LORD.

LAMENTATIONS 3:26

FEW PEOPLE enjoy waiting. We want God's blessings to unfold more quickly so we can enjoy them longer, direction to be given immediately so we can go ahead and make a decision, and conflict to be resolved so we can stop being uncomfortable about it. We're in no hurry to get *past* the good things in life, but we want to get *to* them as soon as possible. And when we're in need—when we have to wait for God to rescue us out of some predicament or solve some problem—the wait can be excruciating.

There are different kinds of waiting. Sometimes we wait because we have no choice; circumstances refuse to move as fast as we want them to, and we respond with anxiety, anger, or manipulation. At the other end of the spectrum, many of us decide there's nothing we can do, and we try to put things out of our mind until they unfold—with no anticipation or participation on our part. To observers, these responses may look like patience, but they aren't. We defer to God's timeline because we have no control over it, though we would take control if we could.

Waiting in faith is different. It is active in anticipation and responsive to God's leading, never pushy or anxious. To some it may look like patience, to others like passivity. But it's really the perfect balance, expecting God to reveal his goodness and partnering with him by faith. Waiting on God is an exercise in trust.

This exercise may stretch us well beyond our comfort level, like when we need to make a decision and guidance is slow in coming, or when circumstances are critical yet God seems slow to intervene. We live much of our lives in the tension between our need and his provision for it.

But that's the point: Those who take matters into their own hands or give up do not trust God; those who wait for him do.

Jesus' followers didn't know they were waiting for a resurrection; they simply thought their hopes had ended tragically. But we've seen the empty tomb, and we know God does his best work when the world has done its worst. His intervention in our lives may seem slow, but it is coming. It comes most powerfully to those who live with anticipation of the morning's new mercies, even in the darkest night.

— PRAYER —

Father, help me live with the kind of patience that expects your provision to come. I choose to anticipate your goodness, your miracles, and your touch. May my faith honor your willingness to give. Amen.

REFLECTION

How does waiting in anticipation of God's goodness honor him? In what circumstances does it stretch our faith?

Further reading: Psalm 30:4-5

He lives to silence all my fears;
He lives to wipe away my tears;
He lives to calm my troubled heart;
He lives all blessings to impart.

"I KNOW THAT MY REDEEMER LIVES," SAMUEL MEDLEY

Thursday

— DAY 14 —

GOD *in the* DARK

LAMENTATIONS 3:31-33

Though he brings grief, he also shows compassion

because of the greatness of his unfailing love.

LAMENTATIONS 3:32

GRIEF CAN BE CATHARTIC, which is why the Bible includes many laments that are not quickly resolved but instead allows those losses to be deeply felt. Our pains cannot be glossed over; they are very legitimate and real. It is good to know the weight of them.

It is not good, however, to let our pain or the world's fallenness grow bitter roots into our souls. Our minds easily lose perspective and exaggerate our grief, forgetting the compassion God gives in the midst of it. No one is abandoned by the

Lord forever (verse 31), but most people who have rejected him have done so because of a gut feeling that he turned his back on them. Behind many seemingly intellectual accusations—claims that he has not given us enough evidence or that he is an absentee landlord—is the pain of an unanswered prayer, a disappointed hope, or a miracle that didn't happen. The human heart longs for his compassion to be made real in the midst of a trial. When it isn't—when God seems distant—arguments against him begin to take root.

Those arguments are made in the middle of the story, when things look grim and the resolution seems unimaginable. But that's the kind of story God is writing. No one is moved by a mild resolution to a mild problem. We applaud a victory in the face of impossible odds. Those moments of crisis are a mark of all good fiction, and they are also a mark of God's best stories. An accusation about God's disappointing absence is the kind of thing a heartbroken disciple might say on the Saturday after the Cross. But the end of the story—in fiction, in God's redemption plan, in our own lives—is coming, and it changes everything.

In the meantime, God shows compassion. We have to

know that. Our laments in this life do not echo off the ceiling; they resonate in his heart, and they draw his attention. He knows what the inside of a tomb looks like. He also knows the story doesn't end there. Yes, our realization of our own brokenness and the world's can be traumatic; so is the Cross, when we come to grips with it. But in the midst of it all, God puts his arms around us, whispers promises about how amazing the end of the story will be, and encourages us to temper our grief with confident hope. In the world's darkest moments and our own, he is there to save.

— PRAYER —

Lord, may my sense of sadness never overshadow your offerings of compassion and hope. You encourage me in the most difficult times. The ends of your stories are always good. Thank you for that truth. Amen.

REFLECTION

If you were one of Jesus' followers during the Crucifixion, what thoughts would you have had about God and his plan? In what ways do you tend to judge God "in the middle of the story" in your life?

Further reading: Romans 8:28-32

He comes the broken heart to bind,
The bleeding soul to cure;
And with the treasures of his grace
To enrich the humble poor.

"HARK, THE GLAD SOUND! THE SAVIOR COMES,"
PHILIP DODDRIDGE

Friday

— DAY 15 —

A CULTURE *of* COMPLAINT

LAMENTATIONS 3:34-42

Who can command things to happen

without the Lord's permission?

LAMENTATIONS 3:37

WHY DOES GOD let bad things happen? It's a common question with an abundance of answers, most with multiple layers. We go through all sorts of theological gymnastics to make sure we keep God and evil separate while maintaining his sovereignty over the world. He doesn't cause evil, yet he is far more powerful than any evil thing. Somewhere in between those anchor points, things get fuzzy.

Still, when bad things happen, the human heart is tempted to accuse him or fate or something else of either allowing these tragedies or singling us out for them. The result is some sort of grievance—usually about circumstances themselves but also with offense toward God. The world is drenched in a culture of complaint against divine orchestration.

We have to discipline ourselves against that. The world carries the bitterness of disappointment, with eyes adjusted to the dark and focusing on everything that's wrong. But we see with new eyes, don't we? We no longer look at the glass as half empty, or even as one percent empty, nor do we see a cross and assume disaster. We look not at what God hasn't done yet but what he has done already and what he has promised to do. That gives us ample reason to live with hearts full of hope and expectation. It also gives us the wisdom to know that hardships don't come because God turned his back. He does not author evil, but he has allowed it for a time. Our trials come with his permission. We are encouraged to overcome them but not to complain about them. God has never botched his dealings with us.

The best remedy against a pervasive spirit is to choose to walk in the opposite spirit. In this case, that means filling your heart and your mouth with praise, even as others around you are filling theirs with discontentment. If our trials come with his permission, then they will work to our advantage. For people who love him, all things do (Romans 8:28). When we remember this, we are freed from the nagging suspicion that God has let us down. At the Cross he proved that he didn't abandon us and never will. That seeming catastrophe turned into the world's greatest blessing. Whatever we face today, we face it with him, not in spite of him. Everything in our lives is given, ordained, intended, allowed—any word that respects God's sovereign will—for a very good reason. Embrace the goodness of his heart in every situation. He is orchestrating your life well.

— PRAYER —

Father, forgive my discontentment. I've often focused on the Good Fridays of my life without seeing the Resurrection Sundays. Thank you for turning every tragic story into good news and every trial into blessing, and help me live with that expectation. Amen.

REFLECTION

Have you ever asked God in frustration, "Why me?" If so, what were the circumstances? How might he have been working those circumstances for your good?

Further reading: Psalm 77

In sickness give us healing,
In doubt thy clear revealing,
That praise to thee be given
In earth as in thy heaven.

"A BRIGHTER DAWN IS BREAKING," PERCY DEARMER

Saturday

— DAY 16 —

A PROMISE *of* RESTORATION

ZECHARIAH 9:9-13

Come back to the place of safety, all you prisoners who still have hope! I promise this very day that I will repay two blessings for each of your troubles.

ZECHARIAH 9:12

ISRAEL HAD a long history of being oppressed by their enemies and eventually defeated by them. Judah's inhabitants had been taken captive into Babylon and dispersed throughout the Persian Empire and beyond. The lamentations of God's people filled their poetry and songs. They were familiar with hardships, disappointments, and heartache. As participants in a fallen world, so are we.

Our instinct is to call out to God. We are told that he is "always ready to help in times of trouble" (Psalm 46:1), and we search the horizons of our lives in anticipation that he will soon step into them with his wisdom, power, and love. The Bible, the resurrection of hope in Jesus, and the many testimonies we have heard have conditioned us to expect his deliverance. We are captive to the promise of his goodness.

God has profoundly encouraging words for captives of hope—those who have lamented the trials and tribulations of life and stubbornly clung to their insistence that he is good. He promises restoration—not just a return to previous conditions, but a double blessing in exchange for the losses of the past. The words of Zechariah offer two blessings for every trouble; Isaiah 61:7 echoes the promise with double honor in place of shame and a double portion of prosperity in land once lost. God demonstrated the principle with Job, who lost everything he had and received twice the recompense in the end. We might question such extravagance, but with God, nothing is too good to be true. The prophets' words were written to people who had suffered the consequences of their own rebellion and sin. The double restoration was promised even to those whose losses were their own fault. God is just that generous.

It isn't unusual for God to give more blessings than we need. There may be delays; he sometimes spends years setting up his "sudden" victories. Abraham, Joseph, Moses, David, and many others had to persist in hope. The angel's announcement of a miraculous birth may have seemed sudden to Mary, but the Messiah had been promised for centuries. Heaven and earth converged in the womb of a young mother at a pregnant moment in history—"when the fullness of time had come" (Galatians 4:4, ESV)—and they converge in the fullness of our times too. The help we need from heaven will certainly come, in double portion. The extravagant promises of God are given for one purpose: to resurrect hope in our hearts. And hope will be fulfilled.

— PRAYER —

Father, may I live not with the skepticism of the world but with the anticipation of your goodness. If a promise seems too good to be true, it might just be because of who you are. Fill me with expectant hope always. Amen.

REFLECTION

What losses would you like to receive "double portion" for? Why is it important to remember that our lamentations have an expiration date, but God's promises do not? How does that encourage you to hope in patience and persistence?

Further reading: Isaiah 61:1-7

Perhaps this sun may be the herald of that Sun that
we expect to rise again today, returned to life.

"LA RESURREZIONE," GEORGE FRIDERIC HANDEL,
WORDS BY CARLO SIGISMONDO CAPECE

THIRD SUNDAY *of* LENT

As for me, I know that my Redeemer lives,
and he will stand upon the earth at last.
And after my body has decayed,
yet in my body I will see God!
I will see him for myself.
Yes, I will see him with my own eyes.
I am overwhelmed at the thought!

JOB 19:25-27

— PRAYER —

Lord, you have heard the laments and regrets of my heart. All of them have moved you; none have confounded you. You have a solution for every problem I will ever encounter, long before I'm even aware I need one. Your greatest solution for my every need is Jesus. I know that's true, even if I don't fully understand the mystery of the Cross. Thank you for your mercy, your healing, and your provision. May my soul bless you and lean into your strength always. Amen.

Our hearts, which first dissolved and floated in grief,
forget the pain and imagine songs of joy;
for our Savior lives again.

"EASTER ORATORIO," JOHANN SEBASTIAN BACH,
WORDS BY CHRISTIAN FRIEDRICH HENRICI (PICANDER)

Monday

— DAY 17 —

THE LAMB WHO TRANSFORMS

JOHN 1:29-34

Look! The Lamb of God who takes away the sin of the world!

JOHN 1:29

WE DON'T HAVE to get very far into the Ten Commandments to realize how often we've broken them. Whether or not we have actually constructed idols, our hearts are inclined toward unworthy loyalties. Whether we have served anything or anyone other than God may not be apparent on the surface, but our conscience knows. Whether we have murdered, committed adultery, stolen, lied, or coveted may not be obvious to the people around us, but our inner impulses betray our facades. If we really got a glimpse of God in all his majesty, with our own souls exposed by his light, we would cry out as Isaiah did, appalled at our uncleanness (Isaiah 6:5). We've been thoroughly tainted by the world's rebellion.

We would like to claim ignorance as an excuse. But God's divine nature and power are visible in creation, and we still choose not to seek him, at least for a time (Romans 1:20). Unawareness is not a good defense with a God who promised to be found. So we are left with our guilt, stuck in our habits, and insistent that "we're only human"—forgetting the high honor of being human and the divine image we were originally given. We really are in desperate, self-inflicted need.

The Incarnation of God and his unblemished sacrifice offer the perfect remedy. The source of life grew up specifically for an appointed time of death. Jesus was resolved in his purpose: He insisted that he *must* suffer terrible things and be killed (Luke 9:22). There was nothing accidental in his crucifixion, no tragic twist of fate that resulted in an untimely death at the hands of executioners. It was "the Lord's good plan to crush him" (Isaiah 53:10). Why?

Because the cost of our rebellion had to be paid. The tide of sin had to be reversed. Death had to die.

That is the inauguration of the new covenant, not the end of it. The Cross did away with the penalty of our sin, but it is more powerful than a legal decree. It actually cleanses us of sin. It removes guilt and transforms lives. It leads to resurrection—a new life untainted by the old. We may spend years learning to see this new life as it is meant to be; eyes coming out of darkness always take time to adjust to the light. But we should never settle for less than the Lamb intended. He transforms us to be like him.

— PRAYER —

Jesus, lead me into the blessings of the new covenant.
Help me understand and experience the fullness of its promise.
Cleanse me and make me new—again and again. Amen.

REFLECTION

How do the death and resurrection of Jesus enable us to live as new creatures? How does the power of the Resurrection separate us from our guilt and sin?

Further reading: Romans 8:1-11

There is a fountain filled with blood
Drawn from Immanuel's veins;
And sinners, plunged beneath that flood,
Lose all their guilty stains.

"THERE IS A FOUNTAIN," WILLIAM COWPER

Tuesday

— DAY 18 —

CLASH *of* KINGDOMS

ISAIAH 53

He was despised and rejected—

a man of sorrows, acquainted with deepest grief.

ISAIAH 53:3

Of course Jesus was despised and rejected. Why wouldn't he be? He came as a spotless being into a contaminated world, the oil of anointing into polluted water, the source of life into an environment of decay, the Son of glory into a vainglorious race. He stood at the front lines of a clash of realms between the culture of God's Kingdom and the culture of the world. There is no détente between such opposing parties. Only one can reign. And at the Cross, the victor seemed clear.

Yes, those hostile to Jesus got their wish. He had challenged the status quo, which was inspiring for those at the bottom end, but a threat to those who benefited from it. So the troublemaker was dispensed with. The problem was handled. The movement was quenched, and the "illusioned" became disillusioned one painful Passover eve.

Jesus did not flee this battle, but neither did he fight it on his adversaries' terms. He remained faithful to the culture of his Kingdom, and they remained faithful to the culture of theirs. Theirs was more aggressive, but his was more effective. To undo our shame, he exposed his face to it. To heal us, he bore excruciating wounds. To give us a crown of beauty for ashes (Isaiah 61:3) and joyful dancing for mourning (Psalm 30:11), he embraced the ashes and mourning. It was an odd battle strategy in the eyes of his opponents and followers, and it seemed ridiculously futile.

Until Sunday. By subjecting himself to the hostile forces of this world and not being undone by them, Jesus stripped them of power. They did their worst, and it wasn't nearly enough. For centuries thereafter, we, his followers, have cast our lot with the despised and rejected, acquainting ourselves with sorrow and grief, and not being undone. We take the punches and lashes of this world, and we resolutely continue with our eyes on the truer Kingdom. We stand with Jesus at the front lines of this clash of realms, our opposition thinking it has defeated us while being completely unaware of its loss two millennia ago, and we declare victory. We may mourn, but we dance. We may get burned, but we see beauty in the ashes. We may look weak, but we are crowned with glory. Just like him.

The Kingdom of God is for the weak, humble, and unlikely, but never for the faint of heart. Stand strong in the midst of a contrary culture and know that you have won.

— PRAYER —

Lord, I don't always feel victorious. But in you, I am. It's a strange victory, invisible to many, but powerful and true. Confirm me daily in this victory. Teach me to dance where I mourn. May I wear the crown of beauty well. Amen.

REFLECTION

As a follower of Jesus, in what ways have you experienced victories that looked like losses? How can you represent the culture of the Kingdom in the world today?

Further reading: Psalm 30:11-12

Up from the grave he arose,
With a mighty triumph o'er his foes.
He arose a victor from the dark domain,
And he lives forever, with his saints to reign.

"LOW IN THE GRAVE HE LAY," ROBERT LOWRY

Wednesday

— DAY 19 —

A COMPREHENSIVE GOSPEL

ISAIAH 53

It was our weaknesses he carried;

it was our sorrows that weighed him down.

ISAIAH 53:4

THE GOSPEL OF SALVATION has often been preached as a remedy for the eternal penalty for our sins. That's a spiritual emphasis that is certainly true, but it leaves out a lot. It means God delivered humanity from a problem many people didn't even know they had, but it says nothing about our daily lives—our relationship issues, our health problems, our work opportunities, our income and debt, and everything else we wrestle with. It does not address the wounds we suffered in the past or the fears we have for the immediate future. All it does—and certainly this is a lot—is relieve our concerns about eternity. But seeing salvation as a spiritual legal decree only comforts us regarding our ultimate destiny. It is an incomplete gospel that seems much too theoretical amid the crises of life.

Jesus emphasized the gospel of the Kingdom, which includes spiritual salvation but also so much more. He spent much of his ministry dealing with people's physical bodies, emotional needs, and urgent spiritual concerns. He promised eternal life, to be sure, but he did not confine his promises to the there-and-then. He was a here-and-now Savior as well, demonstrating the goodness of God in everyday circumstances. He declared that "the time of the LORD's favor [had] come" (Luke 4:19).

There are times when we need God to help us manage the difficulties of life—in marriage and parenting, at work, in academics and training, in the difficult demands others place on us, in our finances and bills, in our physical challenges, in *everything.* And we need him not some day, but now. There are also times when the weight of the world's pain haunts our hearts and feels as if it's going to break us.

According to the fullness of the gospel we've been given throughout Scripture, we can know that Jesus carried all of it—our weaknesses and our sorrows—to the cross. He did not come to deal with only one consequence of the Fall; he came to deal with all of them. We may not experience all of his remedies immediately, and we will still have to deal with problems and pain. But nothing is off limits to his mercy and grace. When we ask him to intervene in anything—regardless of what it is—in some way he will. He comforts and carries, delivers and heals, guides and encourages. The Cross is as comprehensive as his love, and he invites us to bring our entire lives into them both.

— PRAYER —

Lord, I cannot thank you enough for carrying my weaknesses and bearing my sorrows. I depend on you for everything, and you always let me. Thank you for all that salvation includes. Amen.

REFLECTION

Are there any areas in which you've been reluctant to ask God to intervene in your life? What does his sacrifice on the cross demonstrate about his willingness to help?

Further reading: Luke 4:16-21

O believe, my heart, believe:
Nothing will be lost to you!
"RESURRECTION SYMPHONY," GUSTAV MAHLER

Thursday

— DAY 20 —

RECEIVE ALL, GIVE ALL

ISAIAH 53

He was beaten so we could be whole.

He was whipped so we could be healed.

ISAIAH 53:5

HOW THE BEATINGS of Jesus heal us of our wounds may be a mystery to us, but Scripture is clear that they do. We may not be able to explain every instance in which he does not physically heal or materially restore what we've lost, but neither can we explain without the promises of the Cross the times that he does heal and restore. All of our sicknesses and brokenness—spiritual, emotional, mental, and physical—are consequences of our rebellion at the Fall, and Jesus took the pains of that rebellion upon himself. God's character is the basis of his mercy and grace toward humanity, and the Cross is the clearest expression of his character. It is the event through which we receive every good thing from him.

Don't be reluctant to ask and receive—to claim the payment of the Cross for your sins, the healing it brings to your wounds, and the comfort it brings to your soul. The gifts and mercies of God are complete and comprehensive, and you would never want your faith to fall short of what he offers to give you on faith's terms. Ask him to help you experience his saving work to its fullest. That's the kind of prayer he loves to answer.

Having done that, realize that whatever healing and deliverance you've experienced from him immediately qualifies you to be a minister of healing and deliverance for others. What you have freely received, freely give. Everyone on the planet is walking around with wounds from the past, insecurities about the present, and fears for the future, whether they manifest such concerns or not. Many have been healed significantly already; still, everyone needs ministers of grace in their lives. Be one of them every chance you get.

That isn't easy to do. People often try to compensate for

their brokenness and emptiness in ways that offend and alienate. A minister of grace has to be able to see past the offensiveness and recognize the pain inside. The walking wounded of this world need the ministry of the Cross, and the only way for them to get it is to experience it through someone who has already received its healing work. So receive his restoration completely, give it freely, and let the wounds of Jesus do their healing work. Healing is the reason that he came.

— PRAYER —

Lord, may my faith rise to the level of your promise,
and may it not stop when my own needs are met.
Give me opportunities to be a minister of grace to many
of the wounded lives you gave your life to save. Amen.

REFLECTION

In what areas of your life have you experienced healing from Jesus? How does that experience qualify you to minister to others with similar needs?

Further reading: Psalm 103:1-5

Wash thou our wounds in that dear blood,
Which from thy heart doth flow;
A new and contrite heart on all
Who cry to thee bestow.

"ALL YE WHO SEEK FOR SURE RELIEF," LATIN HYMN

Friday

— DAY 21 —

FINALLY FREE

ISAIAH 53

All of us, like sheep, have strayed away.

We have left God's paths to follow our own.

Yet the L*ORD* *laid on him the sins of us all.*

ISAIAH 53:6

HUMAN BEINGS are masters at self-justification. Even though we have ample evidence that we are all fundamentally broken people living in a fundamentally broken world, many of us are reluctant to admit our own sinfulness. So we redefine morality on our own terms and reject any absolutes that contradict them. We easily see the faults of others, and in introspective moments we'll admit our own—to ourselves. But we'd prefer to live in denial, and many of us are very good at it.

Rejecting the idea of sin does nothing to get rid of it, however. Deep inside, we know the world is broken, and we know we're part of the problem. As the prophet Isaiah wrote, we have all strayed like wayward sheep. We've followed our own paths and taken pride in doing things our way. An approach to life that seems normal to us is actually scandalous in the Kingdom of God. He designed us to be like him, and we chose not to. The Father sent the Son to die for our betrayal.

Jesus' death atones for our sin and brings us back from our rebellion, but we have to participate in it by faith and taste its self-denial if we want to leave our fallen nature behind. We can't liberate ourselves, even when we understand the source of our captivity. All we can do is recognize our need and depend on the sacrifice of Jesus to free us. We have no power; we can only participate in his.

Humility and confession are essential keys for participating in his power. While the world tries to get past guilt by denying it, Jesus helps us get past guilt by facing up to it. Go ahead and admit it, he says. All those mistakes we wondered about—those things we hoped were justifiable—really do fall short of our original design. The world says, "How dare you call me sinful!" and stays enslaved. We say, "Yes, I'm that and more," and are set free.

That's the only way to freedom. Strayed sheep cannot maintain their independence and still experience the love and protection of the shepherd. We must recognize our straying tendencies and submit to the shepherd's voice. Every single one of us is wrong about our own inherent goodness but not about our value. That was made clear at the Cross. We are thoroughly loved, forgivable, and destined for divine fellowship. Freely confess your sins, faults, flaws, and weaknesses. Then walk in your freedom from them forever.

— PRAYER —

Lord, I long to be free. I have nothing to hide from you and no reason to impress others. I embrace the freedom of acknowledging my sins and faults. Thank you for cleansing me of them. Amen.

REFLECTION

Do you ever find yourself posturing to be more righteous than you are? If so, how do you think others would respond if you were more open and vulnerable about your weaknesses?

Further reading: Proverbs 28:13

Forbid it, Lord, that I should boast,
Save in the death of Christ, my God!
All the vain things that charm me most,
I sacrifice them to his blood.

"WHEN I SURVEY THE WONDROUS CROSS," ISAAC WATTS

Saturday

— DAY 22 —

THE DIGNITY *of* SILENCE

ISAIAH 53

He was led like a lamb to the slaughter.

And as a sheep is silent before the shearers,

he did not open his mouth.

ISAIAH 53:7

THERE WAS DIGNITY, even majesty, in his silence. No one would be moved by a Savior who insisted on defending himself to the bitter end or made endless appeals to his legal counsel to get out of his predicament. But Jesus simply declared who he was and did nothing to avoid the backlash. He had lived for this moment as a lamb appointed for slaughter. He demonstrated the character of his Kingdom in the face of everything opposed to it.

Observers were stunned. Why didn't Jesus fight back?

Why was he so willing to accept the consequences of his disruption of the status quo? Was his silence an implicit admission of guilt? With so much at stake—he had claimed to be God's Son, after all—why wouldn't he fight for his life or, even more, wield divine power to prove his identity? If he was really who he said he was, why didn't he force his opponents to bend to his will? And if he wasn't, why didn't he act like other would-be messiahs who had tried and failed to rally a movement against the authorities? Why did this Messiah behave so un-messiah-like—and yet remain so godly in his demeanor?

Jesus' silence was necessary to demonstrate the real battle: the ultimate depravity of the world against the pure righteousness of God. Evil versus innocence. Pride versus humility. Earthly power versus divine wisdom. If Jesus had used the same verbal and legal weapons that the government and religious authorities had used, he would have fueled the fire, and the conflict would have turned into a battle of ideas and arguments. But that was not the nature of this battle. It was a conflict of spiritual realms. Jesus' silence was a profound rebuke to the world's ways.

That ought to tell us something about how we conduct ourselves in the world. Our mission as ambassadors of reconciliation is not well served by getting into arguments. Yes, we should explain the truth and defend it, but no one is convinced by words unless divine wisdom and character are behind them. Our task is not to argue the Kingdom but to live it. A battle of ideas wins few hearts. A demonstration of the Kingdom wins many. And it expresses the dignity and majesty of the King.

— PRAYER —

Lord, above all, teach me to be a good reflection of Kingdom values and ways. Let me express your nature. Inspire my words, but even more, inspire my life. Amen.

REFLECTION

Which tends to concern you more: that your words reflect the truth or that they reflect the spirit of God's Kingdom? Why is it important to reflect both?

Further reading: 1 Corinthians 2:1-5

Freely thy life thou yieldest, meekly bending
E'en to the last beneath our sorrows' load,
Yet strong in death, in perfect peace commending,
Thy spirit to thy Father and thy God.

"AND NOW, BELOVED LORD, THY SOUL RESIGNING,"
ELIZA SIBBALD ALDERSON

FOURTH SUNDAY *of* LENT

In Jerusalem, the LORD of Heaven's Armies
will spread a wonderful feast
for all the people of the world.
It will be a delicious banquet
with clear, well-aged wine and choice meat.
There he will remove the cloud of gloom,
the shadow of death that hangs over the earth.
He will swallow up death forever!
The Sovereign LORD will wipe away all tears.
He will remove forever all insults and mockery
against his land and people.
The LORD has spoken!
In that day the people will proclaim,
"This is our God!
We trusted in him, and he saved us!
This is the LORD, in whom we trusted.
Let us rejoice in the salvation he brings!"

ISAIAH 25:6-9

— PRAYER —

Lord, I long for that day when your Kingdom comes on earth in all its fullness, when tears are no more, when death is not only swallowed up in victory but disappears forever. Help me represent that reality in this age, and help me live with hope for the age to come. Amen.

Through this thy prison, Son of God,
must come to us our freedom;
Thy dungeon is the throne of grace,
the refuge of the righteous;
For hadst thou not borne servitude,
would we be slaves eternally.

"ST. JOHN PASSION," JOHANN SEBASTIAN BACH

Monday

— DAY 23 —

FORGIVEN BEFORE WE FELL

ISAIAH 40:1-5

"Comfort, comfort my people," says your God.

"Speak tenderly to Jerusalem.

Tell her that her sad days are gone

and her sins are pardoned."

ISAIAH 40:1-2

THE PROPHET SAW ahead to a time when God's people had been disciplined severely for their sins. History would prove him right; the devastation of Jerusalem and the captivity of its people in Babylon was a catastrophic event and an earth-shaking theological crisis. How could God let his chosen people, the delight of his eye (Zechariah 2:8, ESV), fall to ungodly Babylonians? For years, the people of Judah lived in exile, hung up their harps, and sat down and wept by the rivers of a foreign land (Psalm 137:1-4). Their spirits were crushed.

Long before this cataclysm, Isaiah wrote God's words of comfort to Jerusalem. God spoke tenderly to his precious possession and pardoned its sins. That may seem to us like nothing more than much-needed encouragement and a nice personal touch, but that's because we look back at these words long after the story has already been resolved. When Isaiah wrote this prophecy, God's people had not yet rebelled to the point of judgment, and they could not imagine the suffering that was to come. In other words, God had an answer for their sin long before they needed it. He knew what was going to happen and had already compensated for it. He planned a solution and gave them hope well before they had lost it.

We see a similar pattern in the larger salvation picture. We're told that God loved us and chose us "before the foundation of the world" (Ephesians 1:4, ESV)—before we had sinned, before we were born, before the world had rebelled or even been created. He looked ahead to our need before we existed and planned for it. He was not taken by surprise when we sinned, nor has any decision we've ever made turned him away. He already accounted for our wanderings and had a remedy in place. We were forgiven before we fell.

No wonder the words spoken through the prophet are comforting. They prove that God has not permanently turned away from any of his people. If he had planned a solution before the problem came, then he was not irrevocably offended by the problem. He made a commitment to us that could not be broken by our failure. The Messiah came because God is for us. Our guilt is undone and the weight of it is removed. We can rest in what God has done because he did it for us unconditionally. His delight in his people never fades away.

— PRAYER —

Father, your mercies are unfathomable, and your knowledge of my heart and my need is too deep to understand. Thank you for choosing me, drawing me into your Kingdom, and never letting me go. Amen.

REFLECTION

In what ways is God's foreknowledge of our sin comforting? How do his tender words change our perception of our trials?

Further reading: Ephesians 1:3-8

Oft, oft with weeping eyes
I gaze to heaven;
Then, at your look, arise
restored, forgiven.

"BEFORE THE COCK CREW TWICE," HALLGRIM PJETURSSON

Tuesday

— DAY 24 —

A DEMONSTRATION *of* GOD

ISAIAH 40:1-5

Fill in the valleys,

and level the mountains and hills.

Straighten the curves,

and smooth out the rough places.

ISAIAH 40:4

THE ROUGH PLACES and curves of life serve a purpose. They set the stage for God to reveal himself. He would never have been able to demonstrate that he delivers, for example, without someone having been held captive. He could show no forgiveness unless we sinned or reveal himself as healer unless someone was sick. He could not show unconditional love if there were no possible conditions, nor could he show mercy in a world that never needs it. His attributes of majesty, glory, power, wisdom, and love might be visible under any conditions, but his problem-solving attributes would be forever hidden in a perfect world. So the imperfect came. It had to. The valleys and hills are the backdrop for God's revelation of many of his most beautiful characteristics.

But those valleys and hills do not need to continue forever. God's works in the context of our trials will become an everlasting testimony to his true nature; like trophies on the mantel, they tell a story. But once he is done revealing himself on the stage of our trials—once the story is told—the trials will be resolved. The curves will be straightened and the rough places made smooth. The valleys and mountains of life will be leveled.

This ought to be profoundly comforting for any citizen of the Kingdom of God. We often cry out to God in adversity and wonder why we are having such a difficult time. We forget that the purpose of our mountains and hills, even those of our own making, is to set the stage for a revelation of God—that whether he shows his deliverance, healing, mercy, power, provision, or comfort, he will demonstrate *something* in our distress. And there will come a time when he no longer shows his overcoming nature because there will be nothing left to overcome. Our trials and our sins have an expiration date.

When we become aware of God's purpose, we begin asking a different question in our crises. Instead of, "Why me, Lord?" we learn to ask, "Lord, how do you want to reveal yourself in this situation?" He steps in with some demonstration of his goodness, and he gives us a greater assurance: In the end, the mountains, hills, valleys, curves, and rough places of our lives will be no more. All of our crises will be past-tense testimonies, and our future will be filled with praise.

— PRAYER —

Lord, how do you want to reveal yourself in the rough places of my life? Teach me to expect a demonstration of your goodness in every situation. No mountain is bigger than you; fill my heart with hope for the day when you level each one completely. Amen.

REFLECTION

How has God demonstrated his goodness in the trials of your life? Why are such situations necessary for him to reveal some of his attributes?

Further reading: 2 Corinthians 12:8-10

Be still, my soul: Thy best, thy heavenly Friend
Through thorny ways leads to a joyful end.

"BE STILL, MY SOUL," KATHARINA VON SCHLEGEL

Wednesday

— DAY 25 —

A REVELATION *of* GLORY

ISAIAH 40:1-5

Then the glory of the L*ORD will be revealed,*

and all people will see it together.

ISAIAH 40:5

GOD'S REVELATION of glory has always come in the most unlikely circumstances: at the edge of the Red Sea with no apparent way to cross it; when his people are vastly outnumbered but are singing his praises on a battlefield—in a den of lions or a fiery furnace—and, most surprisingly, on a Roman instrument of torture and death. Looking from the front end of these traumatic events, God's glory seemed to be nowhere in view. On the back end . . . well, we're still talking about what God did to overcome his enemies and rescue his people. In each case, the revelation of glory was so glorious because the circumstances were so dire.

That's how impressive victories work. We applaud a miraculous comeback or a stunning reversal of fortune. The most captivating music is often the most difficult to play. We expect good movies and books to take us to the depths before they take us to the heights. The dawn is most beautiful after the darkest nights. Heroes become heroes in extreme circumstances, not comfortable ones. In other words, glory is best observed in contrast—which means the Cross, that ugliest of deaths, is the perfect stage for an unexpected revelation.

Think about how hopeless things looked as Jesus surrendered his spirit on the cross. His followers had placed all their messianic hopes on him. Many had heard from his own mouth that he was God's Son. In spite of his warnings to the contrary, they set their expectations on some sort of immediate reign in this material realm. They had no sense of where they stood in history or how universal this Messiah would be. Their hopes for their redemption and Israel's deliverance hung bleeding and disfigured on a Roman cross and were then placed in a sealed tomb. Things don't get more hopeless than that.

But no situation is hopeless with God, of course. Impossibilities don't actually represent things that are impossible; they represent opportunities for glory. God's glory was revealed on a cross in Jerusalem nearly two thousand years ago, and it is revealed every time he intervenes in our lives. The greater the difficulty, the greater the revelation.

Remember this the next time you feel hopeless. Your circumstances may not change immediately—though don't rule that out—but if you hold on to faith, God will reveal himself in them eventually. Every life, including yours, is designed in one way or another to become a display of his glory.

— PRAYER —

Father, that's my desire—to be a revelation of your glory. You've demonstrated your goodness time after time, even when my eyes were focused on impossibilities. Display your nature for me, in me, and through me. Amen.

REFLECTION

In what ways did God reveal his glory at the cross? How does he reveal it today?

Further reading: John 1:14

Sing, my tongue, the glorious battle,
With completed victory rife,
And above the cross's trophy,
Tell the triumph of the strife.

LATIN HYMN, VENANTIUS FORTUNATUS

Thursday

— DAY 26 —

THE FELLOWSHIP *of* GLORY

JOHN 17:22-24

I have given them the glory you gave me,

so they may be one as we are one.

JOHN 17:22

THE UNIVERSE and its inhabitants are designed to be a revelation of God's glory. The human race departed from that script in the opening act, but we didn't thwart God's purpose. He revealed his glory through the people of Israel, then through the life, death, and resurrection of Jesus, and now through those who believe in the Son. In fact, the apparent detour we took in our rebellion played perfectly into his plan; it became the essential setting for a fuller revelation of his attributes. His glory shines brightly in a dark world.

God has made it clear that he will not share his glory with idols (Isaiah 42:8; 48:11), but that says nothing about his desire to shine through his people. Idols are God's rivals for worship in the human heart. His people, made and remade in his image, are not. In fact, we are Plan A for his revelation of glory in this age. Jesus made a remarkable statement in his priestly prayer the night before his crucifixion: that he had shared his glory with his followers in order that we might be one with each other and with the Father and Son. It's an invitation for all believers into the unity of the Trinity—the oneness that the Father, Son, and Holy Spirit share is a harmony we can hardly imagine. The Father and Son do not withhold divine glory from others; they share it freely for a clearer revelation of God. The fellowship of glory is a testimony designed to transform the world.

We typically look to God to intervene in the world's problems and provide his solutions, but God looks back to us. His nature was demonstrated in Jesus, and we are now in him. His power works through us. Whether we feel up to the task or not, we are meant to be carriers of the Spirit and manifestations of the Son in this world. The Son is the exact image of God (Hebrews 1:3), and in our regenesis, we are being formed into his image (Romans 8:29). We are pictures of the divine glory.

That's a high calling, and it's easy to be intimidated by it. But God's calling is always beyond our abilities, and his power always accompanies it. Faith allows us to grow into the image of God, and our fellowship with him and his people fills us with the glory we were designed to carry. Through this God fills the earth with a revelation of his nature—just as he intended from the beginning.

— PRAYER —

Lord, you have always called people to tasks that are greater than their abilities and vision. Teach me to step into the fullness of your calling for me. May I be conformed to your image and carry your glory everywhere I go. Amen.

REFLECTION

In what ways do you think God manifests his glory through his people? What part do you play in that revelation?

Further reading: Ephesians 1:11-14

He made the path to glory plain;
Ah, no! He did not die in vain.

"HE DID NOT DIE IN VAIN," CARRIE E. BRECK

Friday

— DAY 27 —

UNSHAKABLE

HAGGAI 2:6-9

This is what the LORD of Heaven's Armies says:
In just a little while I will again shake the heavens
and the earth, the oceans and the dry land.

HAGGAI 2:6

THE WORLD IS SHAKING. You have probably noticed that. The headlines regularly announce convulsions in government, economics, culture, worldviews, and so much more. Fear of the future is rampant, and controversies about how to control it or manage it—or even survive it—seem never-ending. People are searching for solid footing and finding that almost everything moves.

This is nothing new, of course. The world has always been shaking. Entire civilizations have come and gone;

modes of thinking are constantly evolving; styles and trends are fleeting; and all our attempts at security have proven remarkably insecure. But even with a solid perspective on history's patterns, we can sense the tremors accelerating and growing more intense. We don't want to panic, as so many have done in the past, but we also don't want to be unprepared. We have to be able to face the future without fear.

Do not be surprised or dismayed. The shaking is normal. It's the contrast between a transitory material world and an absolute spiritual realm. In this clash of these two kingdoms, so prominent in the themes and reflections of Lent, one is always passing away while the other is always birthing something new. The old can be shattered, but the new can't. That's the way it always has been and always will be until Jesus comes.

God has a purpose in the shaking. It serves to establish his Kingdom in this world. False hopes and securities fall by the wayside as their foundations crumble; only truth remains constant. As hearts go searching for something imperishable, many are drawn to him. He mercifully disrupts humanity's misguided purposes and attachments in order for multitudes to discover their true ones.

You have everything you need to remain unshakable. Jesus assured his followers of that when he urged them to build their lives on his teaching as if they were building a house on solid rock (Matthew 7:24-27). Storms will come and the earth may be shaken, but the rock of absolute truth never moves. In this season of reflecting on the contrasts between the material world and the spiritual world, let the Kingdom of God take center stage. Anchor yourself fully in the eternal realm of the spirit, and no amount of shaking will be able to move you.

— PRAYER —

Lord, my heart is at rest in you because I have chosen to build my life on the truth of your Word and the certainty of your grace. Thank you that my security does not depend on my faithfulness but on yours. Anchor me always in your love. Amen.

REFLECTION

In what ways have you observed the world's shaking during your lifetime? How does your response to this dynamic distinguish you from those around you?

Further reading: Hebrews 12:25-29

His oath, his covenant, and blood
Support me in the whelming flood;
When every earthly prop gives way,
He then is all my hope and stay.

"MY HOPE IS BUILT," EDWARD MOTE

Saturday

— DAY 28 —

A PURE PRIESTHOOD

MALACHI 3:1-4

He will sit like a refiner of silver,

burning away the dross.

MALACHI 3:3

MALACHI PROPHESIED at a time when Judah's priesthood needed a reformation. Many of God's people had come back from exile to rebuild Jerusalem and the Temple, and while the religious leaders had reinstituted old patterns of worship and sacrifice, they had become apathetic in their commitment to God and corrupt in their practices. Traditions and memories of a vibrant priesthood under David and Solomon persisted, and contemporary moods seemed much less zealous by comparison. The prophet spoke of God's desire for renewal. God himself would come to his Temple like a blazing fire that burns the dross out of precious metals to purify them. If anyone could stand at his appearing, it would be only by his grace.

This purge of priestly impurity may come across to us as an ancient concern, but it's extremely important to the Messiah's mission. Jesus came not to do away with the priesthood but to expand it. Where one tribe of Israel had once presided over the nation's religious life, now every believer serves as a priest—a representative who stands at the intersection of heaven and earth, appointed to represent God to human beings and human beings to God. We have become a nation of priests (1 Peter 2:9; Revelation 1:6), filled with the holy presence of God in order to hear confessions (James 5:16), declare forgiveness (John 20:23), and intercede for each other (1 Timothy 2:1; Ephesians 6:18). Our ministry in the Messiah's name is meant to accomplish what the Messiah himself came to do. We love, heal, deliver, teach, exhort, encourage, and more. We are messengers of a new and lasting covenant.

God wants pure messengers. His desire for a pure priesthood did not end when the Temple in Jerusalem was destroyed. It applies to all believers—those who serve in his priesthood today. True purity, of course, means sinless perfection, and while we don't have that inherently in ourselves, we do have it in the Messiah. It is given to us as a gift; we can claim Christ's ministry and purity as our own. Our job now is to step into the image of God that has been restored to us—to grow into what has already been declared true. The more our life aligns with our identity, the more power and weight our priesthood carries. The zeal of the Lord ignites the zeal of his people as we minister in a transient, shaking world.

— PRAYER —

Lord, let me blaze with your holy zeal. Transform how I see myself. Open my eyes to my position as a priest between heaven and earth who represents you to others and others to you. May I reflect your character and your passion well. Amen.

REFLECTION

To what degree have you seen your life in Christ as a priesthood? In what ways have you received priestly ministry from others? How does awareness of that mutual role affect how you relate to people?

Further reading: 1 Peter 2:9-12

O Christ, look with favor upon your faithful people
Now gathered here to praise you;
Receive their hymns offered to your immortal glory;
May they go forth filled with your gifts.

"CANTIQUE DE JEAN RACINE," GABRIEL FAURÉ

Fifth Sunday *of* Lent

How beautiful on the mountains
are the feet of the messenger who brings good news,
the good news of peace and salvation,
the news that the God of Israel reigns!
The watchmen shout and sing with joy,
for before their very eyes
they see the LORD *returning to Jerusalem.*
Let the ruins of Jerusalem break into joyful song,
for the LORD *has comforted his people.*
He has redeemed Jerusalem.
The LORD *has demonstrated his holy power*
before the eyes of all the nations.
All the ends of the earth will see
the victory of our God.

ISAIAH 52:7-10

— PRAYER —

Lord, my life is shaped by the things I hunger for, and you have blessed me with a longing for the things of heaven. Continue to stir up my hunger for the good news of your Kingdom. Rebuild the ruined places of my life, and strengthen the gifts and calling I have already received. Let me be a revelation of your goodness, grace, and glory that I might live as part of your promise to display your victory to the ends of the earth.

Christ to all the world gives banquet
On that most celestial meat,
Him, albeit with lips most earthly,
Yet with holy hearts we greet,
Him, the sacrificial Pascha,
Priest and victim all complete.

BYZANTINE HYMN, SAINT ANDREW OF CRETE

Monday

— DAY 29 —

THE NEW FEAST

REVELATION 21:1-7

The one sitting on the throne said,

"Look, I am making everything new!"

REVELATION 21:5

SOME PEOPLE came to Jesus one day and asked him why his followers did not fast like the followers of their religious leaders and John the Baptist (Luke 5:33-39). Jesus did not dismiss fasting by any means, but he made a remarkable statement about timing. His followers sensed that they were with the bridegroom and ate like they were at a wedding feast. They were, even in their limited understanding, celebrating a new covenant, a new relationship, and an entirely new kind of life.

Jesus compared the new life he offers to a new wineskin. Old and new skins can't be sewn together because an old container is rigid and the new skin will expand. New life can't be imposed on old structures; the new creation can't blend with the ways of the world. The follower has to choose between religious traditions and spiritual renewal. One caters to our understanding and comforts us with predictable patterns; the other stretches our faith and sends us on an exciting but somewhat nerve-testing adventure. The new does not conform to old paradigms and will ultimately break them. But it is definitely worth celebrating.

Lent is a good time to fast in prayer and repentance, but that kind of solemnity is a marker and memorial of our transition from old to new, not the substance of the Kingdom life. No, the Kingdom life is a wedding feast, a celebration of the newness that came with the Resurrection. We are a different kind of creature, no longer born merely of this world but of another realm. We plant our feet not in the fallen world of Genesis but in the regenesis of a greater creation. Why? Because our essence has changed. We are butterflies leaving the remnants of our caterpillar life. We are not who we used to be.

Mourn the fallen condition of the world and your own soul, but do not remain in that state for long. Anticipate the Resurrection—a departure from past brokenness and the entryway into a thoroughly new existence. Whenever your experience seems to point you back toward the old rather than into the new, insist that your life line up with the promise of the gospel rather than the other way around. Your inheritance, by God's own promises in the old covenant and fulfillments in the new, is for rebirth. Look at his movements in your life. Feast on them. He really is making all things new.

— PRAYER —

Jesus, you are the template for my new existence. I no longer look to my old ways of life; I look to you. Create in me a new heart, a new vision, a new joy. Lead me into Kingdom ways, and help me lead others into them too. Amen.

REFLECTION

Are there times when life seems old, stale, and predictable? According to God, what is the reality of your condition? What practical steps can you take to walk in newness of life?

Further reading: Isaiah 43:18-19

Again the Lord of light and life
Awakes the kindling ray,
Unseals the eyelids of the morn,
And pours increasing day.

"AGAIN THE LORD OF LIGHT AND LIFE,"
ANNA L. BARBAULD

Tuesday

— DAY 30 —

HOPE BEHIND *the* CLOUDS

MATTHEW 16:13-23

From then on Jesus began to tell his disciples plainly that it was necessary for him to go to Jerusalem. . . . He would be killed, but on the third day he would be raised from the dead.

MATTHEW 16:21

PETER HAD JUST come to a staggering realization about Jesus' true identity not only as the Messiah but as the Son of the living God. To Peter and the other disciples, that identity surely sparked visions of glory, hopes for the redemption of Israel, and the nation's restoration to an independent Kingdom where God could reign and draw people from all across the lands to Jerusalem's Temple. Such glory had been prophesied for Israel long ago (Zechariah 8, for example), and now the time seemed to be at hand. This Jesus really was the long-awaited Messiah and King.

It made perfect sense, then, when Jesus turned his attention toward Jerusalem (verse 21). This quest marks a key moment in Luke's Gospel as Jesus set his face toward the holy city (Luke 9:51), as though nothing could deter him. To the disciples, his resolve surely confirmed their hopes—until Jesus began explaining what would happen there. Jesus foretold terrible events, including his own death. He mentioned the Resurrection, too, but who could absorb a mysterious comment like that with the idea of a tortured and defeated Messiah still ringing in their ears? No, this could not happen, Peter insisted, as he rebuked the Son of God he had just affirmed. The Messiah simply cannot die.

But in God's plan, the Messiah was sent exactly for that reason. The Incarnation served to reset the template for humanity and pay the price for our rebellion. This death was the only way to inaugurate life; you can't overcome something by ignoring it. Jesus faced the brunt of sin's consequences face-to-face, reversed the direction of history, and superimposed a Kingdom of life and growth over the remains of death and decay. Both streams are evident today, but only one will last. And it began with something that looked like the end of hope.

You won't always understand God's plan in your life—in fact, you may be surprised if you ever do—but you can be certain it makes sense to him and works out well for you. He often does his best work undercover, perhaps to keep our best intentions from interfering, as Peter tried to do. In God's eyes, it's far more important for you to believe than to understand. What looks to you like the end of hope may actually be hope's beginning. And death—of God-given bodies, hopes, and dreams—is never the end.

— PRAYER —

Lord, my circumstances often look contrary to your purposes for my life, and I don't always understand why. But I trust you, and I cling to that trust daily. It's all I've got. And according to your Word, it is enough. Amen.

REFLECTION

Why do you think God's plan so often seems shrouded in dead-end circumstances? How have you seen this pattern play out in your life?

Further reading: Romans 4:18-22

The rosy morn has robed the sky;
The Lord has risen with victory:
Let earth be glad, and raise the cry,
Alleluia.

"THE ROSY MORN HAS ROBED THE SKY,"
NICOLAS LE TOURNEAUX

Wednesday

DAY 31

THE EVIDENCE *of* LIFE

JOHN 11:1-44

Didn't I tell you that you would see

God's glory if you believe?

JOHN 11:40

THERE WERE SIGNS of the revelation of glory before Jesus came out of the tomb. Not long before his crucifixion, Jesus received word that his friend Lazarus was sick. Rather than rushing off, he remained on the other side of the Jordan for two more days—a wise move in the eyes of his disciples who, as much as they loved Lazarus, recalled the danger Jesus had faced back in Judea, where Lazarus lived. So when Jesus said he wanted to go wake Lazarus up (verse 11), the disciples were alarmed. He informed them that Lazarus had died, and it was time to prove a point. "For your sakes, I'm glad I wasn't there, for now you will really believe" (verse 15). Jesus was pretty blunt about their misperceptions.

Lazarus became an early symbol of Easter, and in keeping with the symbolism, Jesus was intentionally "late." He let despair enter into the hearts and minds of his friends and followers before he relieved them of it. In the face of death, he declared himself to be "the resurrection and the life" (verse 25)—not that he *gives* resurrection and life but that he *is* resurrection and life. Everyone who lives in him and believes in him (verse 26) participates in his life, which is full of joy and never ends.

We might assume such good news would be universally welcomed, but the resurrection of Lazarus resulted in a death plot against Jesus (John 11:53) and eventually a death plot against Lazarus, too (12:10), as he was living, breathing evidence of the new creation. That's because the guardians of the world system will try to kill any evidence that threatens its power structure, even when the power structure oversees nothing but futility and decay. In the mind of a world ruler, the glory of God takes a back seat to his or her own. It's a ridiculously worthless trade made repeatedly on our planet every day. And it keeps people from awakening to the glory God willingly shares.

Whatever it costs to your own dreams or expectations, embrace the glory of God fully and walk in it daily. No matter how dark things look, believe. Always see the hope behind the clouds. The taste of God's promise may not have remained for long—eventually Lazarus died again—but the promise itself certainly remains. The glory is both a present reality and a forever hope. The Kingdom has come, is coming, and will fully come when Jesus returns. And we are invited to experience it fearlessly, by faith, every day.

— PRAYER —

Lord, how can I experience your Kingdom more fully? Show me the ways. Give me eyes of faith to see what you are doing behind the scenes and to participate in it. Make me unexplainable to the world. Amen.

REFLECTION

The night before his crucifixion, Jesus said, "Now the Son of Man is glorified and God is glorified in him" (John 13:31, NIV). How is God glorified in such a dark and tragic event? How does this challenge our concept of glory?

Further reading: 1 John 2:15-17

Make us more than conquerors,
Through thy deathless love;
Bring us safe through Jordan
To thy home above.

"THINE IS THE GLORY," EDMOND L. BUDRY

Thursday

— DAY 32 —

THE END *of* FRUITLESSNESS

MATTHEW 21:18-22

I tell you the truth, if you have faith and don't doubt, you can do things like this and much more. You can even say to this mountain, "May you be lifted up and thrown into the sea," and it will happen. You can pray for anything, and if you have faith, you will receive it.

MATTHEW 21:21-22

JESUS SAW A FIG TREE with no fruit on it and cursed it—a seemingly capricious act from a very patient Savior. But there was a lot of symbolism in this cursing, as well as a teaching moment for the disciples. As the fig tree withered away at Jesus' words, it signaled judgment on a fruitless generation and the world's ways. It also marked the end of an age of futility. No longer would humanity have frustration and fruitlessness as its only option. A corrupt local leadership and a wider world of brokenness had met their conquering King. The death and decay of the Fall were being usurped by a greater reality. Inspired words could now wield authority over a world of sorrow.

How? By the power of faith. Jesus made the fig tree an object lesson for his astonished disciples. Not only would they be given authority to speak words of faith over fruitlessness; they would also be able to move mountains. Jesus could point to enormous obstacles—in this case, most likely Herod's fortress on a man-made hill within view from the fig tree—and tell his followers to pronounce judgment on them. The ways of the world have to surrender to the decrees of the insistently, stubbornly, relentlessly faithful. Sometimes the results are immediate, as Jesus demonstrated with the fig tree, but our experiences prove that the battle and the wait can often be long and arduous. Nevertheless, the words and prayers of faith eventually triumph. The new creation always takes precedence over the old.

When we look for evidence of that victory in specific moments or situations, even our new eyes may strain to see it. But if we persist in our faith against the tyranny of surface appearances, and if we look at how the Kingdom has grown over the course of history, we can see how victorious our words and prayers have been. The fig tree was emblematic of the fruitlessness of human effort independent of God. Our earthly, kingdom-building ambitions and maneuverings do not produce the fruit of God's Kingdom. Faith in the Messiah and his authority do.

Let go of old, fruitless paradigms. It's time for them to wither away. Newness and life are contained in the words of Jesus and, by extension, in the Spirit-inspired words of his followers. Wield them often, be persistent, and watch mountains move. You now live in a Kingdom of unearthly ways and uncommon fruitfulness.

— PRAYER —

Lord, teach me the ways of your Kingdom. Fill my mouth with powerful words of faith that accomplish your purposes. May the fruitless places in my life wither away and the glories of your Kingdom come. Amen.

REFLECTION

What does Jesus' cursing of the fig tree say about his priorities? What does it teach his followers about fruitfulness?

Further reading: 1 John 5:4-5

Against the foe in vales below
Let all our strength be hurled;
Faith is the victory, we know,
That overcomes the world.

"FAITH IS THE VICTORY," JOHN H. YATES

Friday

— DAY 33 —

A HEART *in* SYNC *with* HIS

JOHN 12:1-8

She did this in preparation for my burial.

JOHN 12:7

NOT LONG BEFORE Mary of Bethany anointed Jesus' feet, she had directed a very pointed question at him: "Lord, if only you had been here, my brother would not have died" (John 11:32). Her grief and the weeping of others made him angry—not at her or them, but at the devastation of death that had long ravaged humanity. Jesus could have kept Lazarus from dying, of course; observers watching this scene accused him of missing an opportunity to do just that (John 11:37). But as we have seen, Jesus knew what he was doing and how he would reveal his glory in this tragic situation. Mary took note. Her doubt at Lazarus's tomb turned into faith as Jesus approached his own.

No one else seemed to be convinced that Jesus meant what he said about dying in Jerusalem. But Mary, seemingly aware of the meaning of her actions, took an expensive bottle of nard perfume and anointed Jesus with it. Whether she knew the significance or not, he certainly did. She was preparing him for burial, he said. She was displaying her devotion in the face of the world's fickleness, her affirmation before the time of his abandonment, her belief in the power and life of Jesus' words even in the time of his death. Her heart was going with him to the grave.

That's the highest possible justification for our Lenten focus on the temporality of this age. We are connecting our hearts to Jesus and letting him take us with him to the grave. We are not in denial about the fleeting nature of this world, and we have no illusions about escaping it. No, we face the Cross and death in full knowledge that we, with him, will overcome. The way out of this broken world is not in fleeing from it but in going through it. When we do that wrapped up in the unquenchable life of the divine Son, we inevitably come out unscathed.

We can't physically anoint Jesus for burial as Mary did, but we can submit our hearts to the path of his obedience. While most of the world aims for an upward trajectory, we know the only way up is to go down. We humble ourselves, we carry a cross, and we enter the tomb with Jesus. Buried with him, we come out in his resurrection—fully alive, healed and whole, victorious and unassailable. The world would never have figured out this path, but like Mary, we listened to Jesus. His words have set us free.

— PRAYER —

Lord, I know that if my heart is with you in death, it remains with you in life—flourishing, growing, fully alive with joy. Bind me to yourself in every way, that I might experience your life in every way. Amen.

REFLECTION

How does our focus on the temporality of this age connect us with Jesus' mission at the cross? How does it deepen our experience of the resurrection?

Further reading: Colossians 2:9-15

Awake, O heart, the morn is bright,
All doubt and fear is o'er!
The Lord is ris'n in power and might,
He lives forevermore!

"AWAKE AND SING," ALICE JEAN CLEATOR

Saturday

— DAY 34 —

THE GREATER EXODUS

LUKE 9:28-36

Behold, two men were talking with him, Moses and Elijah, who appeared in glory and spoke of his departure, which he was about to accomplish at Jerusalem.

LUKE 9:30-31, ESV

IT WAS A DRAMATIC SCENE, surely part of what impressed John to write, "We have seen his glory" (John 1:14). Jesus had taken three of his closest disciples to a mountaintop, and the visible layer of this physical realm was peeled back to reveal the dazzling image of the Son and two holy heroes of ages past, Moses and Elijah. The revelation of glory was undeniable in that moment, and the scene was loaded with significance. Two of the greatest figures of Hebrew history were conversing with the Son of God. What were they talking about? According to Luke's Gospel, they were discussing the departure—literally, the exodus—that was about to take place.

Most translations of the Bible assume the topic to be Jesus' own exodus from this world, which would certainly pique the interest of Elijah, whose departure was far outside the norm (see 2 Kings 2:11-12). But an even more meaningful translation suggests that Jesus was talking with Moses and Elijah about the exodus he would soon accomplish on behalf of God's people—an exodus that would connect him with the mission of Moses, who led Israel out of Egypt, across the Red Sea, and to the edge of the Promised Land. It was a nation-defining Exodus that revealed God's glory to Israel many centuries earlier. But the exodus that would soon take place in Jerusalem would be global in scale and would reveal God's glory in an unprecedented and eternally unique way to realms both physical and spiritual. The first Exodus, as miraculous and dramatic as it had been, was only a picture of the one Jesus would accomplish. These key players in God's plan certainly had a lot to talk about.

The radiance of God's glory had shone on Moses' face and

appeared at Elijah's ascension. Now that same holy radiance shone through Jesus at his resurrection and ascension, signaling the ultimate victory of the new creation. Glory would no longer grace a few scattered heroes as a hint of something new. It would fill the bodies, hearts, minds, and spirits of all who believe. The Resurrection was not an exclusive event; it was the first fruit of things to come.

Jesus has accomplished an exodus for you. It is not an escape from the world, but it is certainly an escape from the world's captivity. You live now as a citizen and ambassador of another realm, bringing heaven's environment into earth wherever and whenever you can. And you, too, will appear with him in glory.

— PRAYER —

Father, may your radiance not only shine on me, as it did with Moses, but shine through me as it does with Jesus. The exodus of Jesus has set me free; may I live freely indeed. Amen.

REFLECTION

In what ways was the Exodus led by Moses a foreshadowing of the exodus led by Jesus? What symbolism is common to both?

Further reading: Hebrews 3:1-6

It was a strange and dreadful strife
When life and death contended;
The victory remained with life,
The reign of death was ended.

"CHRIST JESUS LAY IN DEATH'S STRONG BANDS,"
MARTIN LUTHER

Palm Sunday, Sixth Sunday *of* Lent

As Jesus and the disciples approached Jerusalem, they came to the town of Bethphage on the Mount of Olives. Jesus sent two of them on ahead. "Go into the village over there," he said. "As soon as you enter it, you will see a donkey tied there, with its colt beside it. Untie them and bring them to me. If anyone asks what you are doing, just say, 'The Lord needs them,' and he will immediately let you take them."

This took place to fulfill the prophecy that said,

"Tell the people of Jerusalem,
'Look, your King is coming to you.
He is humble, riding on a donkey—
riding on a donkey's colt.'"

The two disciples did as Jesus commanded. They brought the donkey and the colt to him and threw their garments over the colt, and he sat on it.

Most of the crowd spread their garments on the road ahead of him, and others cut branches from the trees and spread them on the road. Jesus was in the center of the procession, and the people all around him were shouting,

"Praise God for the Son of David!
Blessings on the one who comes in the name of the LORD!
Praise God in highest heaven!"

MATTHEW 21:1-9

— PRAYER —

Jesus, may my praises never be as fickle as those of the crowds in Jerusalem that day. When you come riding into my life, in all the humility of a true King, I will bless your appearance and let go of my expectations. I give you full freedom to reign in my heart, my relationships, and my circumstances. Blessings on the one who comes in the name of the Lord.

All glory, laud, and honor
To you, Redeemer, King,
To whom the lips of children
Made sweet hosannas ring.
You are the King of Israel
And David's royal Son,
Now in the Lord's name coming,
The King and Blessed One.

"ALL GLORY, LAUD AND HONOR," THEODULF OF ORLÉANS

Monday

— DAY 35 —

A ZEALOUS, JEALOUS LOVE

MATTHEW 21:12-17

The Scriptures declare, "My Temple will be called a house of prayer," but you have turned it into a den of thieves!

MATTHEW 21:13

JESUS HAD DEMONSTRATED an affinity for the Temple early in his life. When he was twelve, his parents thought he was with them in the caravan leaving Jerusalem after Passover. Realizing he was missing, they went back to search for him and eventually found him conversing with religious scholars in the Temple. Jesus was astonished that they might have looked anywhere other than his Father's house (Luke 2:41-51). But this time, in the week before his death, he surprised his audience with more than his words of wisdom. He disrupted those who were making a business out of sacrifice and overturned their tables. He demonstrated that the Prince of Peace could be fiercely angry and disturb the peace. His zeal for his Father's house (John 2:17) took a forceful turn.

We shouldn't be surprised by Jesus' anger. He looked with anger at religious leaders when their hard hearts tried to get in the way of his compassion (Mark 3:5). He declared woe on hypocrites who drove people away from the Kingdom of heaven and killed its messengers (Matthew 23:13-33). Here, he blasted the profiteers of worship who turned offerings into a business venture. God's Temple is a place of prayer for the nations, he insisted, quoting the prophets to prove his point (Isaiah 56:7). The religious leaders were stunned by the intensity of his reaction.

Why was Jesus so passionate about these things? Because he reflected the heart of the Father for his people. The passion he demonstrated at the Temple wasn't about the building; it was about the worshipers who had gathered and, on a larger scale, the nations represented by them. Apparently, God isn't just mildly interested in the hearts of human beings. He's fiercely protective of them. He's zealous for our worship and jealous for our love.

We might be tempted to assume that Jesus' zeal for his Father's house no longer applies. After all, the Temple was destroyed within a generation of his resurrection. No one has been changing money there for almost two millennia. But the Father still has a temple that is designed as a place of prayer. It's the human heart and the fellowship of believers (1 Corinthians 3:16-17; 6:19; Ephesians 2:21). We are the temple of his presence. The building gave way to the body a long time ago, and God continues to be passionate about the place of his presence. The purity and prayerfulness of his dwelling place deeply matter to him. He enters our hearts with zeal to drive out unholy influences and make us his own.

— PRAYER —

Father, may I be as zealous for your presence as you are for mine. Thank you for the intensity of your love. Grant that I would learn to love with the same kind of passion. Amen.

REFLECTION

What feelings are provoked in your heart when you think of the intensity of God's passion for you? In what ways can you prepare yourself as his dwelling place?

Further reading: Zechariah 8:1-2

Amazing love! How can it be
That thou, my God, should die for me!
"AND CAN IT BE, THAT I SHOULD GAIN?" CHARLES WESLEY

Tuesday

— DAY 36 —

POWER *in* HUMILITY

JOHN 13:1-20

I have given you an example to follow.

Do as I have done to you.

JOHN 13:15

THE NIGHT BEFORE his crucifixion, Jesus made a remarkable statement by washing his disciples' feet. It was a commendable and surprising act of service that his friends initially resisted—they felt that he, as Master, should not put himself in such a position. But when he insisted and they realized he meant it as a picture of their cleansing, they complied. He told them to follow his example and serve others as well.

That alone is a worthwhile picture, but Jesus was also painting a portrait his followers would not understand until much later. Philippians 2:5-11 tells us how he emptied himself of his divine privileges in order to live as a man, took the form of a servant, lived in obedience—even to the point of death—and then was exalted. When he washed his disciples' feet, he acted out this stunning trajectory by taking off his normal clothing and wearing the towel of a servant (verse 4), meeting the needs of sinful human beings by cleansing them, then clothing himself again in his original attire, and sitting down as though his job were finished (verse 12). In one simple act—one of his last on earth—Jesus manifested the sacrifice he had already embraced in the spiritual realm. He left behind the privileges of Godhood; as a human being, his power came through dependence on the Father. He came to serve.

That act of service and many others were an affront to the spirit of the world. The pride that prompted and fueled human rebellion cannot grasp such selflessness. Jesus overcame our self-centeredness with his humility—a counterintuitive tactic in this clash of kingdoms, but a fitting one. And it was effective, too. His humility took him to the cross as his enemies kept offending and kept assuming their aggression would win the battle. They had no idea that they were reinforcing the character of the Kingdom and the King, and that they were playing perfectly into the divine plan. His capacity to suffer was far greater than their ability to destroy.

If you want to overcome the world, use the weapons you already know: faith, love, wisdom, prayer. But also use the weapons of humility and service. Enemies don't know what to do with that. God does. It becomes his opportunity for meeting needs, changing hearts, and demonstrating the power of his love.

— PRAYER —

Jesus, following this example runs against my nature, but I know it will conform me to yours. Give me opportunities to serve others and demonstrate the humility and power of your love. Amen.

REFLECTION

How does humility serve as a weapon in the clash of kingdoms? How does it overcome the pride of the world? How does service demonstrate God's nature?

Further reading: Philippians 2:5-11

Was it for crimes that I have done,
He groaned upon the tree?
Amazing pity! Grace unknown!
And love beyond degree!

"ALAS! AND DID MY SAVIOR BLEED," ISAAC WATTS

Wednesday

— DAY 37 —

ALL *for* JOY

MARK 14:32-42

He became deeply troubled and distressed. He told them, "My soul is crushed with grief to the point of death. Stay here and keep watch with me. . . . Keep watch and pray, so that you will not give in to temptation."

MARK 14:33-34, 38

THIS WASN'T the first time that human beings in a garden faced temptation. We recall that story from the earliest pages of Scripture, and it did not end well. On the surface, this one would not end well either; one disciple betrayed Jesus, and the others fled the scene. Jesus had told them to stay awake and pray so they would be able to resist, but he, too, had to resist an overwhelming urge to depart from the divine plan. His resistance was enough to overcome this temptation. The Father's plan would proceed without the Son compromising obedience.

This was no stoic experience, however. Jesus was deeply troubled and distressed—"crushed with grief," he told his friends, even "to the point of death." The writer of Hebrews tells us that "while Jesus was here on earth, he offered prayers and pleadings, with a loud cry and tears, to the one who could rescue him from death" (Hebrews 5:7). Whether or not that applies to other occasions of prayer, it certainly applies to this one. The Cross would be an exceedingly painful and traumatic experience—physically, emotionally, and probably most of all, spiritually—and the Son of God was not reluctant to admit it.

Jesus did not submit to the suffering because of some robotic sense of self-control, nor did he quench his passions simply because it was the right thing to do. He fully felt the weight of sin and pain and displayed his anguish outwardly. But another feeling was even stronger: joy. According to the writer of Hebrews, Jesus was able to look past this excruciating moment and see what it would accomplish. "Because of the joy awaiting him, he endured the cross, disregarding its shame" (Hebrews 12:2). His aversion to the coming agony counted for less than his anticipation of the coming glory. Even in the most distressing of circumstances, he could keep his priorities straight.

Life will give us ample opportunities to make the same choice. Superficial gratification now or deeper gratification later? No pain, no gain; or pain for the gain we desire? Self-indulgence or self-discipline? The pleasures of the world or the joys of the Kingdom? These aren't easy decisions, but the choices that line up with the culture of God's Kingdom lead to fulfillment. They reveal which citizenship we most value and which realm we are investing our lives in. And they make us a lot like Jesus.

— PRAYER —

Lord, many times I have prayed, "Not my will but yours." I haven't always said it with joy, but I want to. I believe the joy of fulfilled promises exceeds the pleasures of the moment. Help me make the right choices in every area of my life. Amen.

REFLECTION

On what occasions have you had to choose between present pleasures and future joys? Which do you tend to choose more often?

Further reading: Hebrews 12:1-4

Go to dark Gethsemane,
Ye who feel the tempter's power;
Your Redeemer's conflict see,
Watch with him one bitter hour.
Turn not from his griefs away;
Learn of Jesus Christ to pray.

"GO TO DARK GETHSEMANE," JAMES MONTGOMERY

Maundy Thursday

— DAY 38 —

A DIFFERENT REVOLUTION

MARK 14:43-52

Am I some dangerous revolutionary,

that you come with swords and clubs to arrest me?

MARK 14:48

JESUS HAD BEEN teaching openly for days, and no one laid a hand on him. The political and religious authorities apparently did not want to risk their popularity in front of the crowds, at least not yet. But in the dark of night, when no crowds were there to protest, they came with the betrayer to put an end to this miracle-working nuisance. They came fully armed against an unarmed man.

"Am I some dangerous revolutionary?" Jesus asked with more than a hint of sarcasm. Violent extremists were not unusual in this Roman-occupied land, but Jesus did not fit the stereotype. Of course he was not a revolutionary—at least, not like that. But in the realm of the spirit, where the clash of kingdoms was coming to a head in a garden near Jerusalem, this was a revolution of the highest order. The instigator and orchestrator of the human rebellion, the "ruler of this world," was being cast out (John 12:31; 14:30). Jesus was leading a divine resistance against the ways of the world and the enemies of his Kingdom. He was offering a lasting alternative to a culture of false worship, selfishness, hate, greed, lust, manipulation, and deceit. He knew exactly what was going on behind the scenes, and it was bigger than a handful of contentious Romans and Jews against a teacher and his ragtag group of disciples. Jesus was surely no danger to the political and religious leaders. But to the spirit of the age? Yes—a thousand times, yes. He came to overthrow the existing order.

This is a different kind of revolution, of course—not one that uses physical weapons or military strategies but character and beliefs. It involves planting seeds of kindness and compassion and watching them grow. It employs weapons of humility and prayer to overcome the aggression of the enemy. It involves commitment and sacrifice, just as any good cause does, and sometimes death. But this revolution aims first at the spiritual condition of human hearts and minds, and then at the restoration of more tangible blessings. It isn't like the human rebellion against God; in fact, it moves in exactly the opposite direction. But it is revolutionary just the same.

Invest your life in this revolution, whatever it costs. Maintain your composure in the face of unreasonable hostility. Your kindness and compassion unnerve the forces of darkness. Insist on the character of the Kingdom in every area of your life, and refuse to be moved. The light of God's Kingdom always overcomes.

— PRAYER —

Lord, I gladly join this resistance against the kingdom of darkness. Make me a subversive threat to every spiritual force hostile to you. May your Kingdom come in my life and in my world daily. Amen.

REFLECTION

How might seeing yourself as a revolutionary against the world's ways motivate you to live differently? Why are weapons like compassion and mercy effective in this resistance movement?

Further reading: 2 Corinthians 6:1-10

The strife is o'er, the battle done;
The victory of life is won;
The song of triumph has begun. Alleluia!

"THE STRIFE IS O'ER, THE BATTLE DONE," LATIN HYMN

Good Friday

— DAY 39 —

WHEN DARKNESS FALLS

LUKE 23:44-49

When all the crowd that came to see the crucifixion saw what had happened, they went home in deep sorrow.

LUKE 23:48

THE STORY OF JESUS the Messiah did not end on that Passover Friday so many years ago, but virtually all observers assumed it had. They did not have centuries' worth of Easter celebrations to give them hope. They were not anticipating a resurrection on the third day. They watched in stunned helplessness as Roman soldiers brutally manhandled the body of an innocent man. They witnessed his moment of death and saw a soldier confirm it with the point of a spear. They saw the darkness and felt the earth shake, and some expressed awe and remorse. But no one, as far as the Gospels tell us, sensed any lack of finality. Jesus was dead, and their hopes died with him.

There are moments in life when all we see are pain and disappointment, with no answers in sight. We are encouraged to hope in God's goodness anyway, but he knows how difficult hope can be. He understands our pain and the thoughts we entertain in the midst of it. In the Incarnation, he experienced all the discomforts and sufferings we can experience. Jesus hungered, thirsted, wept, gasped for air, shouted in pain, bled, and died. He was a man of sorrows, fully acquainted with grief, just like many of us. God incarnate entered into the suffering that fallen humanity had brought upon itself, and at the most excruciating moments on the cross, he felt thoroughly, desperately forsaken.

What do you do in those disorienting seasons of life when your pain speaks louder than your hope? Where else do you go when you've turned to the highest authority in the universe and heard only silence? Where do you find consolation when the Consoler's body is lying in a tomb? This is where grief does its deepest work. He always wants to deliver us from despair, but sometimes he lets grief linger. It connects us with his heart as a grief-stricken Father or betrayed Bridegroom. It reveals something of his nature—and sends us in search of joy.

Joy really does come in the morning (Psalm 30:5)—not always in the morning of our choosing, but it does eventually come. Friday is not the end of the story. Hope is never lost, no matter how far gone it seems. There is a balm for pain and disappointment, and healing is on its way.

— PRAYER —

Lord, my heart has wounds that remain unhealed, and you are my only hope. I have made judgments about your goodness between the Fridays and Sundays of my life, and I repent. Forgive me, heal me, restore my hope in your name. Amen.

REFLECTION

Try to imagine how you would have felt as someone who had invested all your hopes in Jesus and then watched him die. What questions would you have for God? What do you think it would take to allow you to hope again?

Further reading: Psalm 22:1-8

Were you there when they laid him in the tomb?
Oh, sometimes it causes me to tremble, tremble, tremble.
Were you there when they laid him in the tomb?

"WERE YOU THERE," AFRICAN AMERICAN SPIRITUAL

Holy Saturday

— DAY 40 —

DARKNESS, SILENCE, *and a* BREATH

MATTHEW 27:57-61

Joseph took the body and wrapped it in a long sheet of clean linen cloth. He placed it in his own new tomb, which had been carved out of the rock. Then he rolled a great stone across the entrance and left. Both Mary Magdalene and the other Mary were sitting across from the tomb and watching.

MATTHEW 27:59-61

IN THE BEGINNING, after God created the earth, it was formless and empty. Darkness covered the deep, and the Spirit of God—literally, his breath or his wind—hovered over the surface. The world was lifeless, and the Spirit/breath/wind brooded, waiting for the word to be given. God shaped the dust of the ground into human form. He breathed his life into the form—"inspirited" it—and a new kind of creature reflected his image. As we know, humanity rebelled, distorting the image and forfeiting the fullness of life. But the breath remained, waiting for the Spirit to hover and brood again. One day, after eons of creation groaning for its redemption, he would.

The earth may not have been formless and empty that Saturday after the Cross, but it might as well have been. Darkness covered the hearts of those who had hoped. Life lay dead in a tomb. The Spirit may have hovered over the surface of broken hearts, but the word had not yet been given to enter in. God was preparing the earthen vessels of his image to receive his breath again. One genesis had set this world in motion; the regenesis would restore what was lost and fulfill what had always been planned.

No one knew this yet on that Passover Sabbath. God was awfully, achingly silent that Saturday. Like the surface of the deep so many ages before, the world seemed lifeless. But only a few days later, just as God had come face-to-face with the first earthen form of a man, a risen Messiah would stand face-to-face with his followers and breathe his Spirit into them

(John 20:22). The long-awaited moment of regenesis finally came. The Spirit/breath/wind blows where it wishes (John 3:8), and it wished to enter into human flesh anew because the Resurrection had secured a new kind of life. In a very real sense, humanity was reborn. So was its hope.

This is where we now live—in a second genesis, a climate of hope where the breath of God is freely imparted to earthen vessels of faith. The things we have mourned are passing away. Yes, the dust returns to dust, but the spirit returns to Spirit. The temporal submits to the eternal. Darkness gives way to light. Death gives way to life. And the creativity of God is flourishing again in the recreated citizens of his Kingdom.

— PRAYER —

Lord, I can scarcely understand what you have accomplished in the genesis of the new creation, but I want to participate in it fully—your breath in me, your vision as my calling, and your Kingdom as my hope. Thank you for making it all possible in the death and resurrection of Jesus. Amen.

REFLECTION

In what ways does the resurrection of Jesus and the impartation of his Spirit echo the first creation? What are the implications of this picture for how we live and see ourselves?

Further reading: John 20:19-23

O Lord of life, desiring
Thy glory now to see,
Beside thy cross expiring,
I'd breathe my soul to thee.

"O SACRED HEAD, NOW WOUNDED," PAUL GERHARDT (ADAPTED FROM BERNARD OF CLAIRVAUX OR ARNULF OF LEUVEN)

EASTER SUNDAY

Early on Sunday morning, as the new day was dawning, Mary Magdalene and the other Mary went out to visit the tomb.

Suddenly there was a great earthquake! For an angel of the Lord came down from heaven, rolled aside the stone, and sat on it. His face shone like lightning, and his clothing was as white as snow. The guards shook with fear when they saw him, and they fell into a dead faint.

Then the angel spoke to the women. "Don't be afraid!" he said. "I know you are looking for Jesus, who was crucified. He isn't here! He is risen from the dead, just as he said would happen. Come, see where his body was lying. And now, go quickly and tell his disciples that he has risen from the dead, and he is going ahead of you to Galilee. You will see him there. Remember what I have told you."

The women ran quickly from the tomb. They were very frightened but also filled with great joy, and they rushed to give the disciples the angel's message. And as they went, Jesus met them and greeted them. And they ran to him, grasped his feet, and worshiped him.

MATTHEW 28:1-9

— PRAYER —

Lord, my words are not enough. My heart is speechless but full of truth, longing but full of joy, free but captivated by the power of your amazing love. May my soul bless your name today and forever. Amen.

Oh, that with yonder sacred throng
We at his feet may fall!
We'll join the everlasting song,
And crown him Lord of all!
We'll join the everlasting song,
And crown him Lord of all!

"ALL HAIL THE POWER OF JESUS' NAME,"
EDWARD PERRONET

You have been given an

opportunity to reveal the character

and nature of God to the world.

Let the light shining in your heart

scatter its rays into other

hearts around you.